devilishly detailed

mandalas and patterns

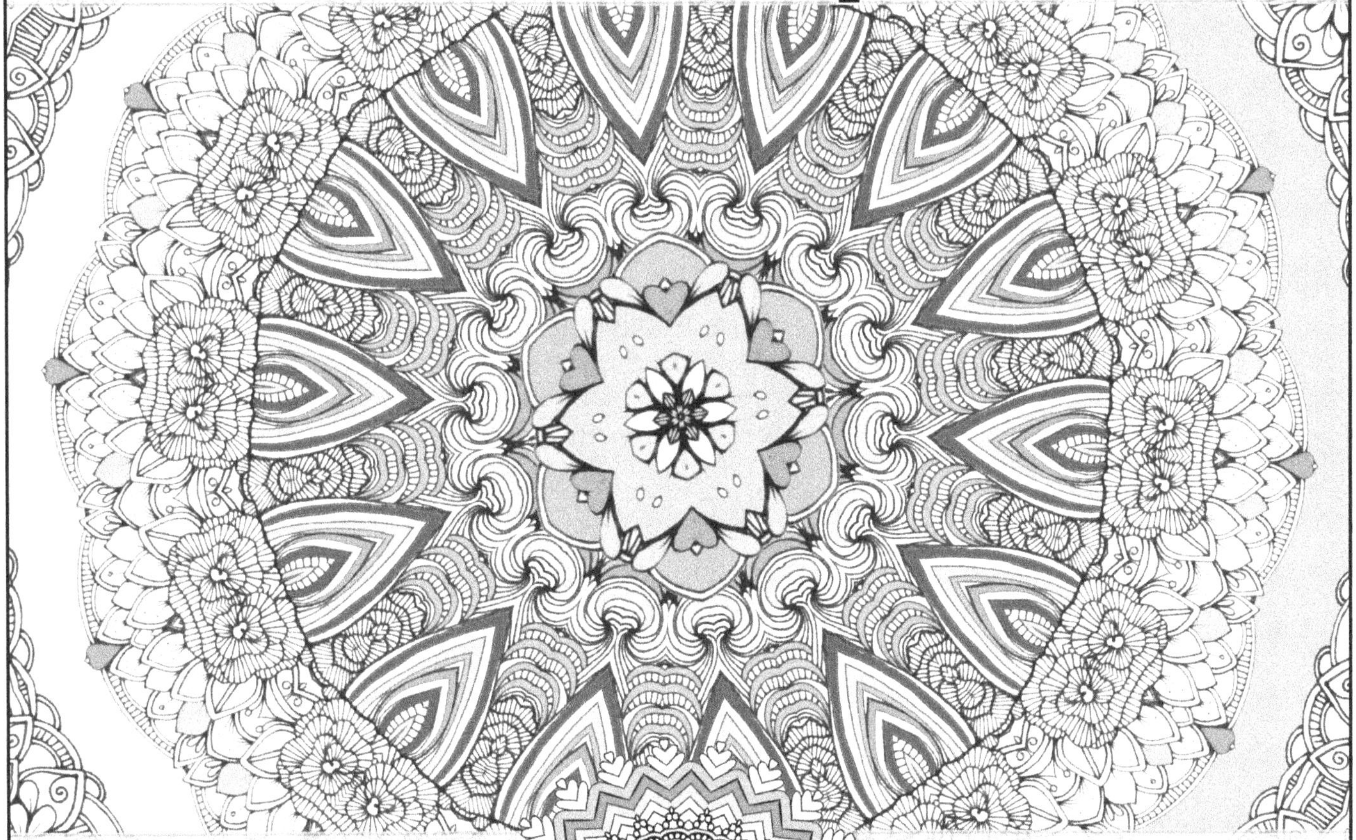

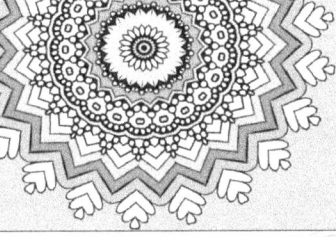

OVER 30 DESIGNS!

EXPERT LEVEL COLORING

Misty McDivitt

VOL. I

Hillbilly Art
5333 Fort Henry Drive
Kingsport, TN 37663
www.facebook.com/hillbillyartcoloringbooks
hillbillyart77@outlook.com

Printed in the United States of America

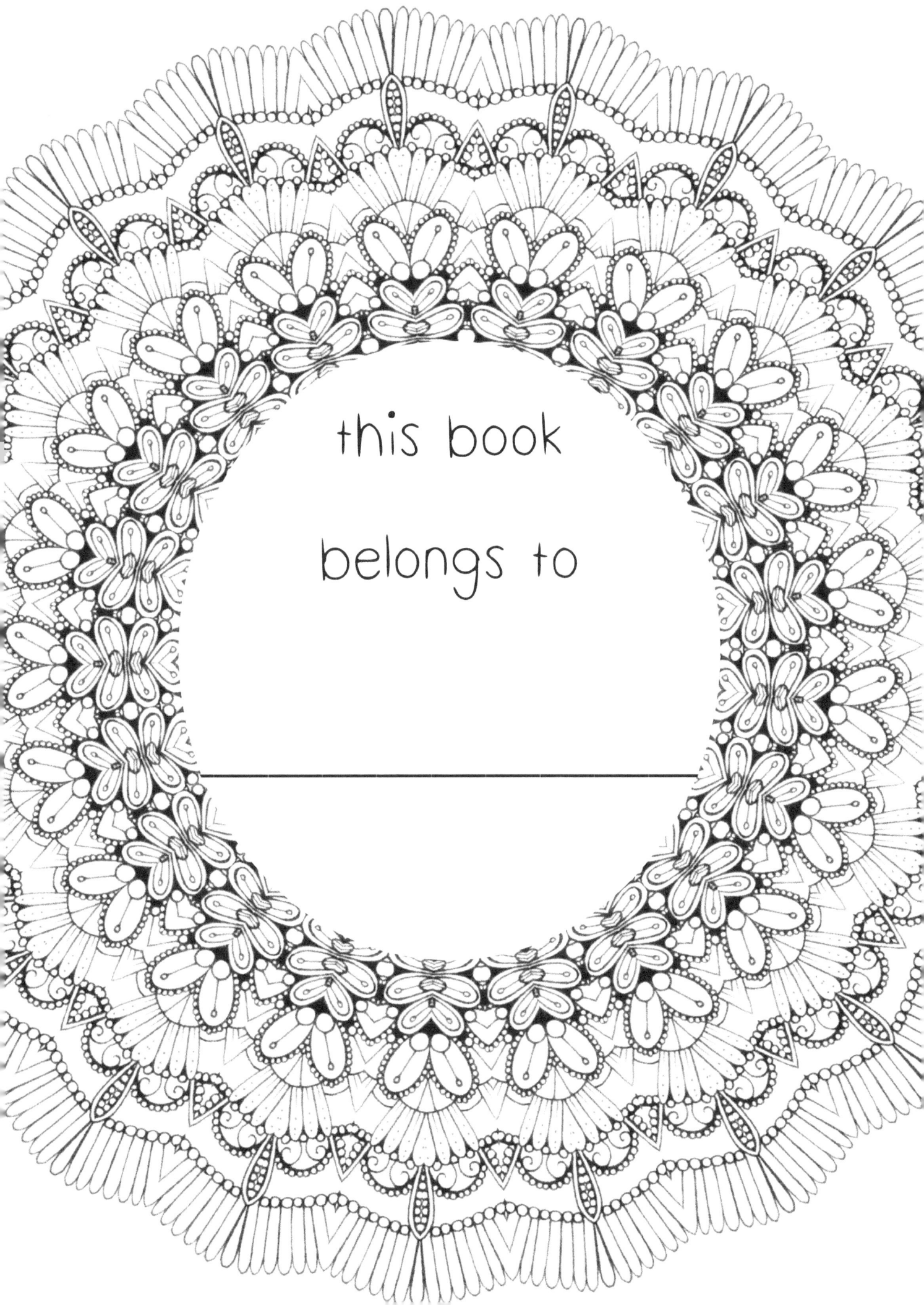

this book

belongs to

_____

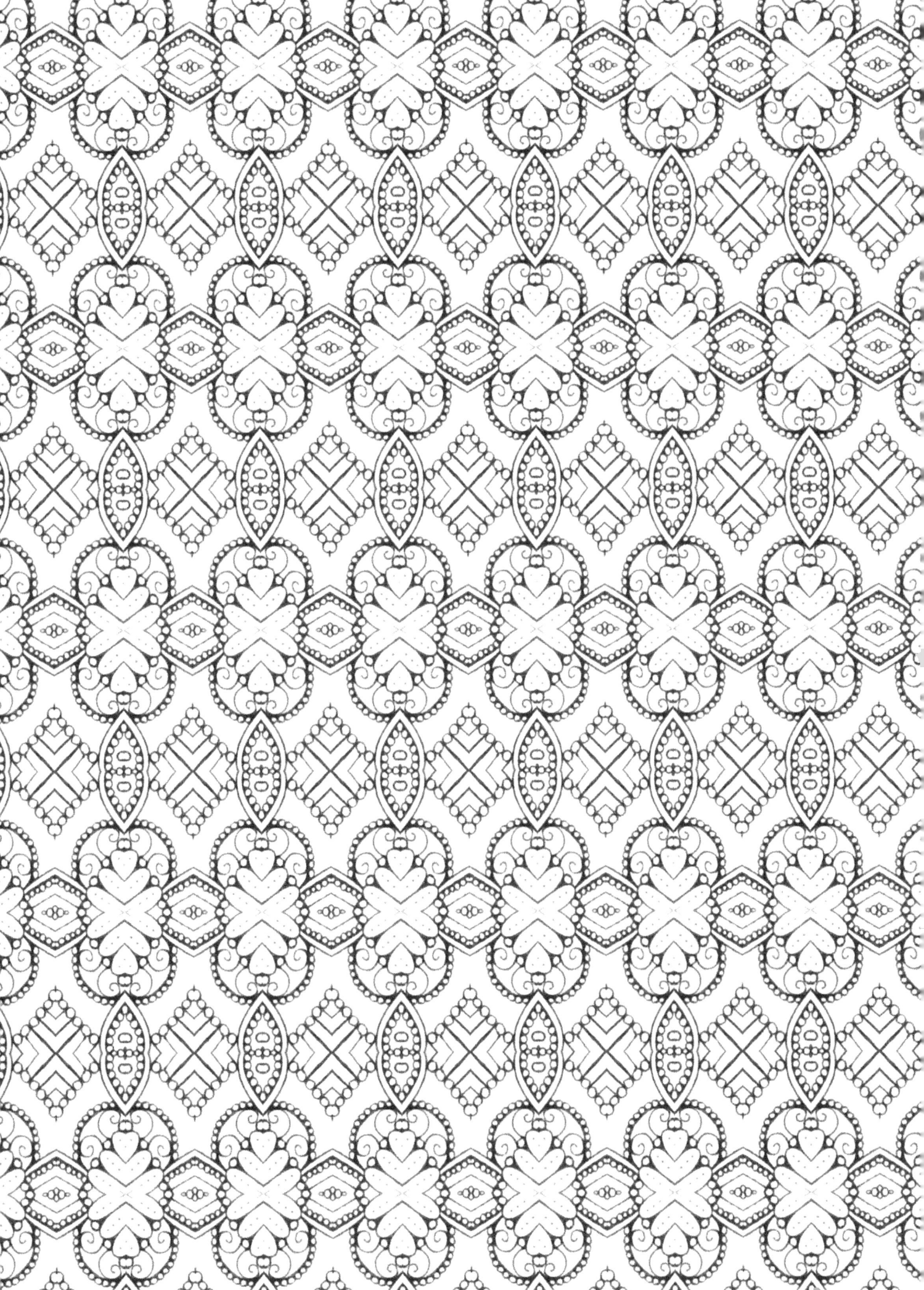

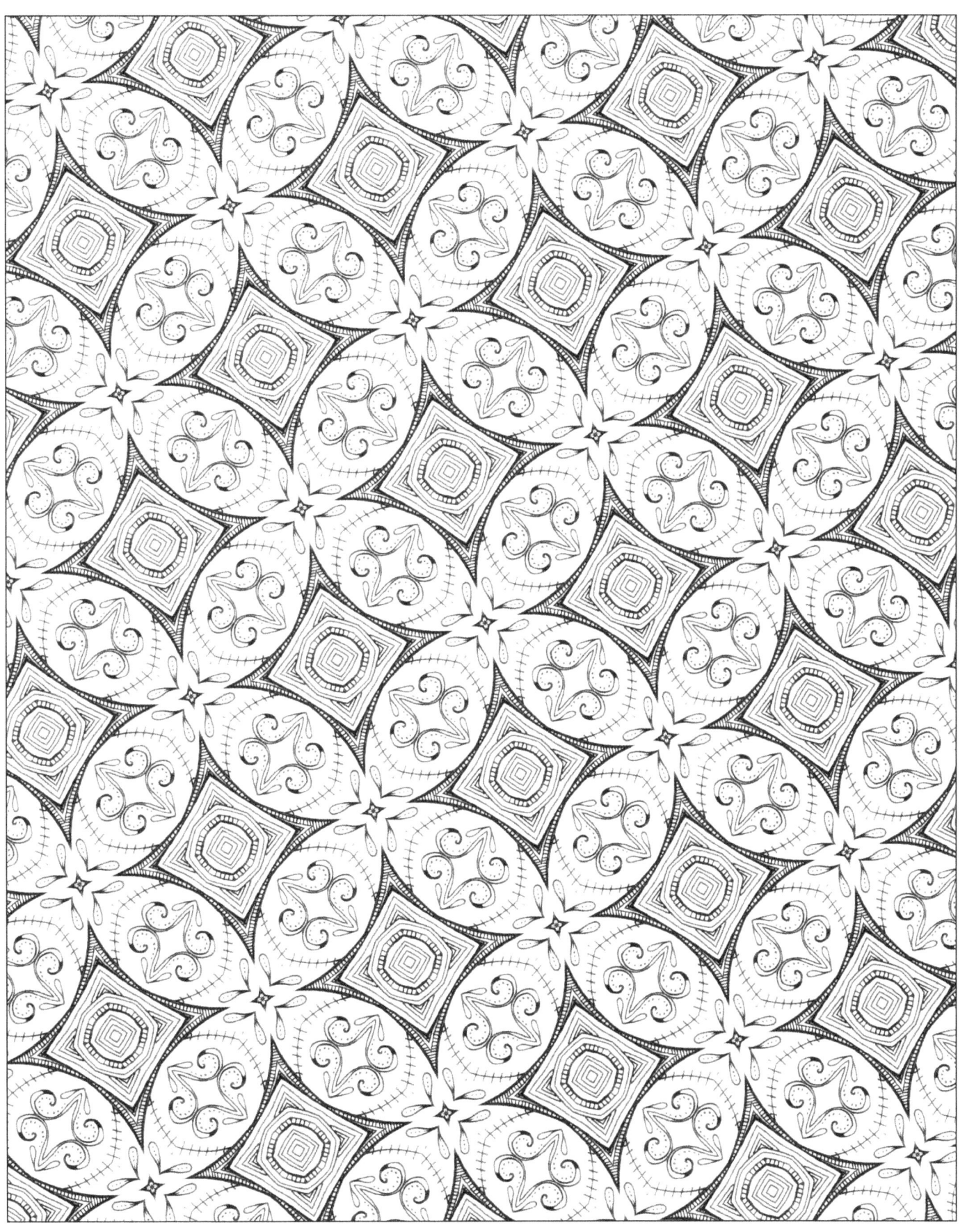

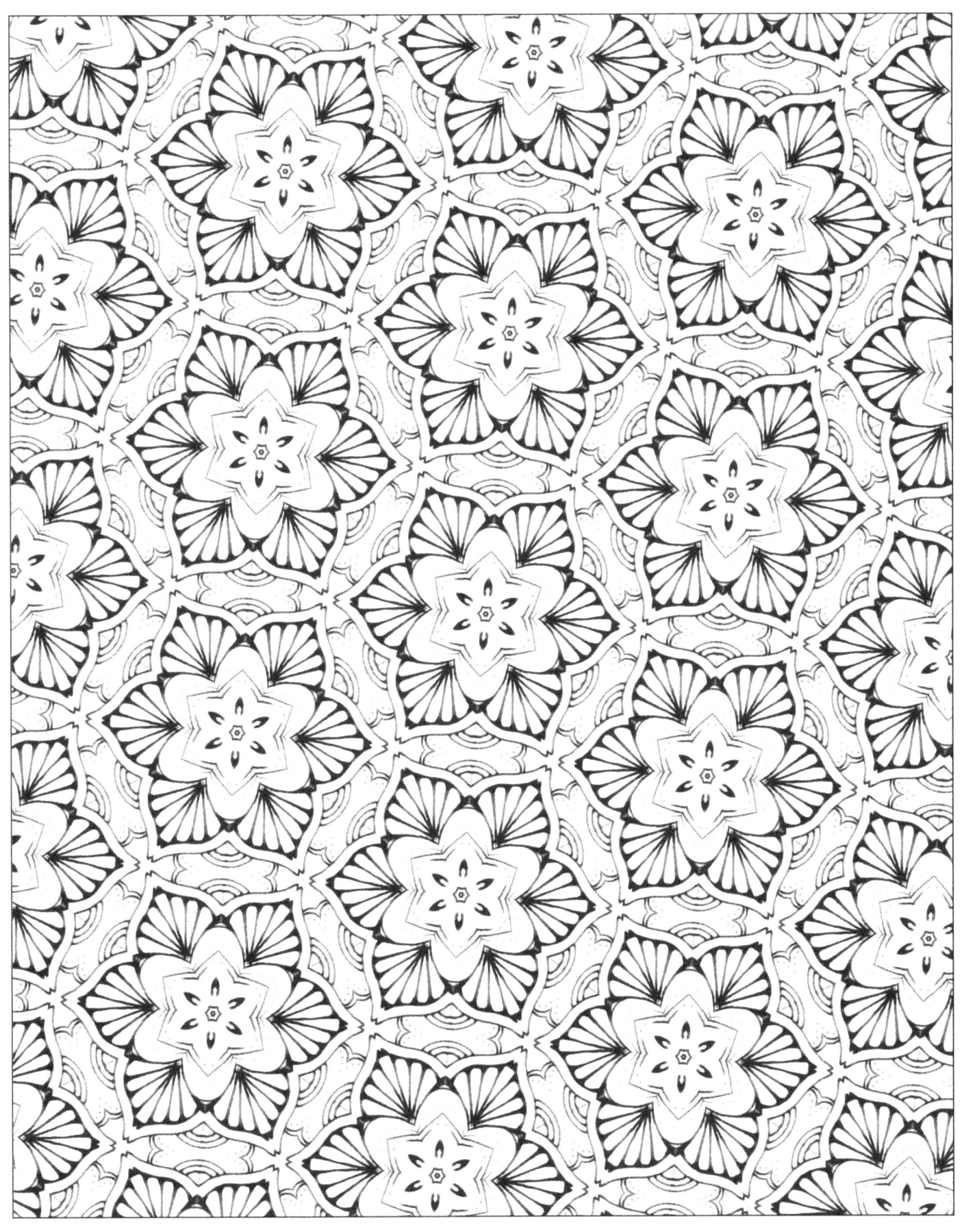

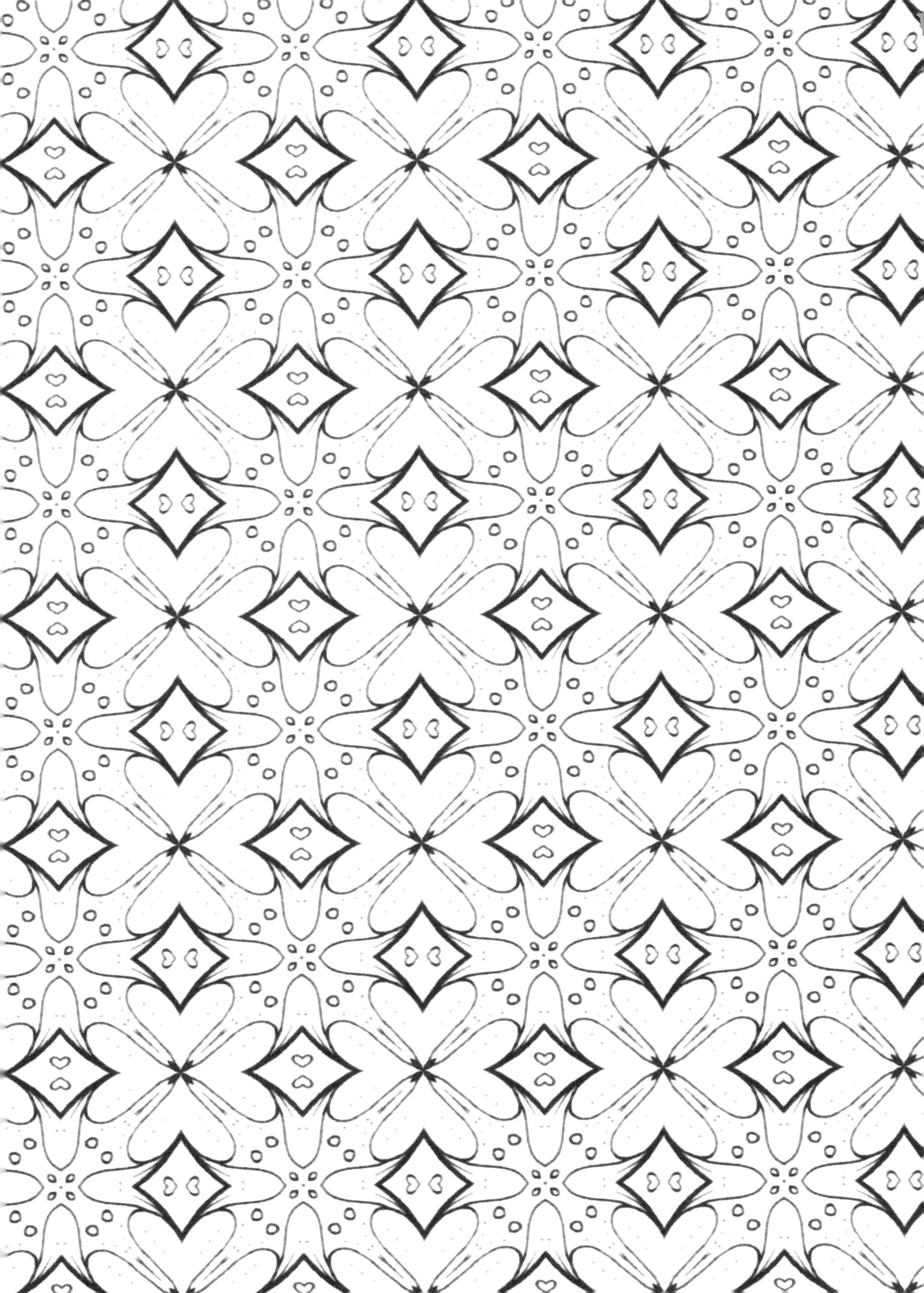

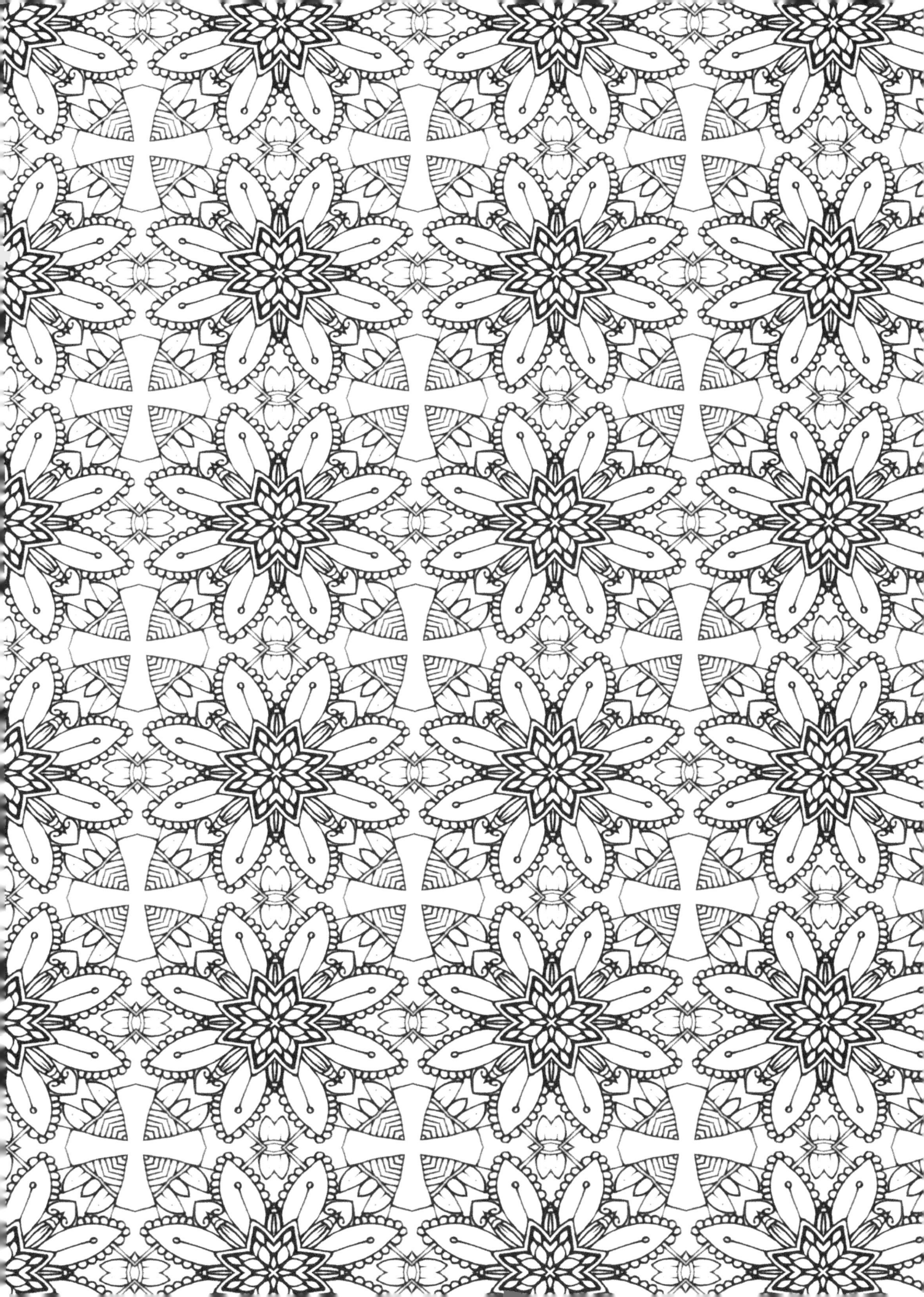

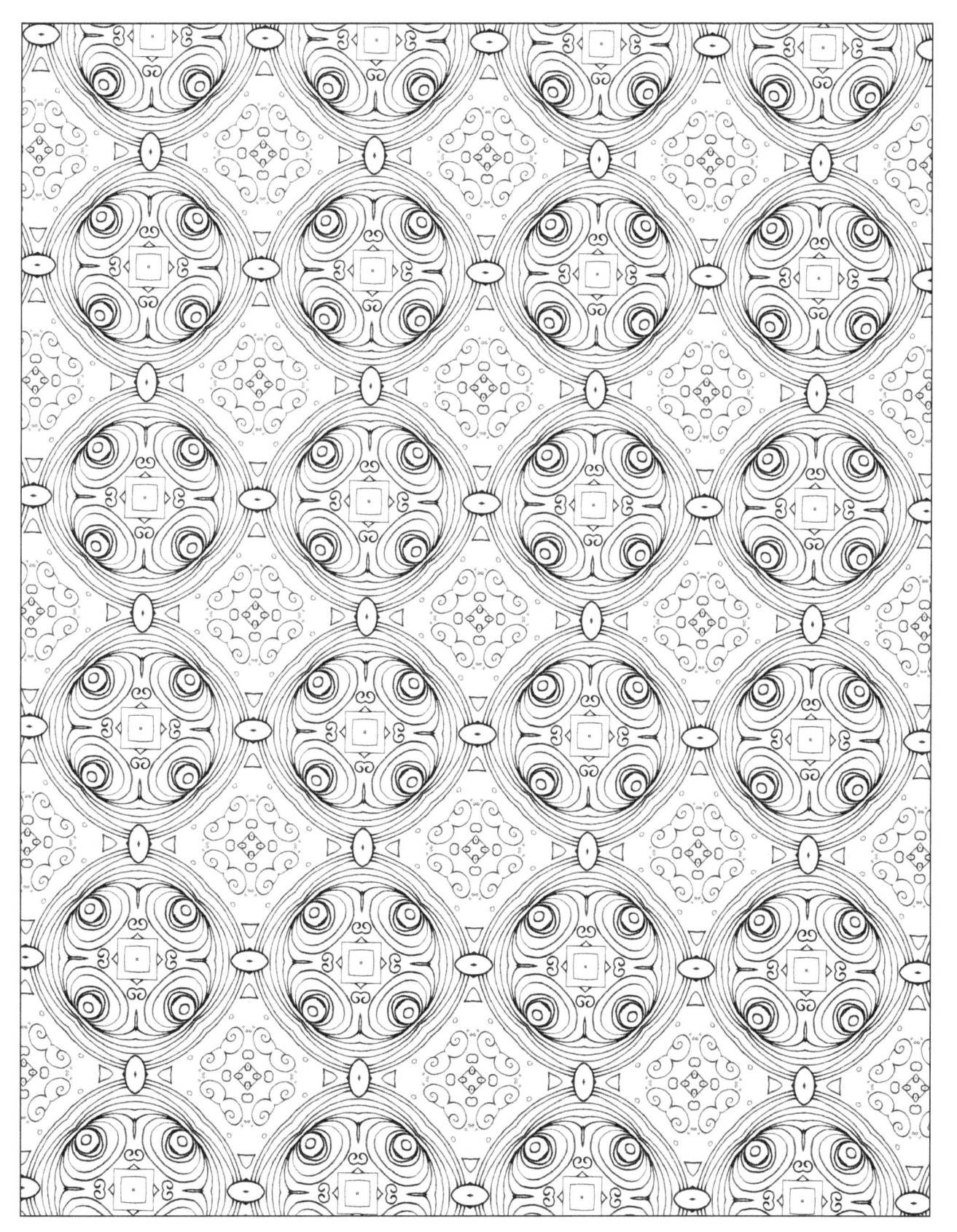

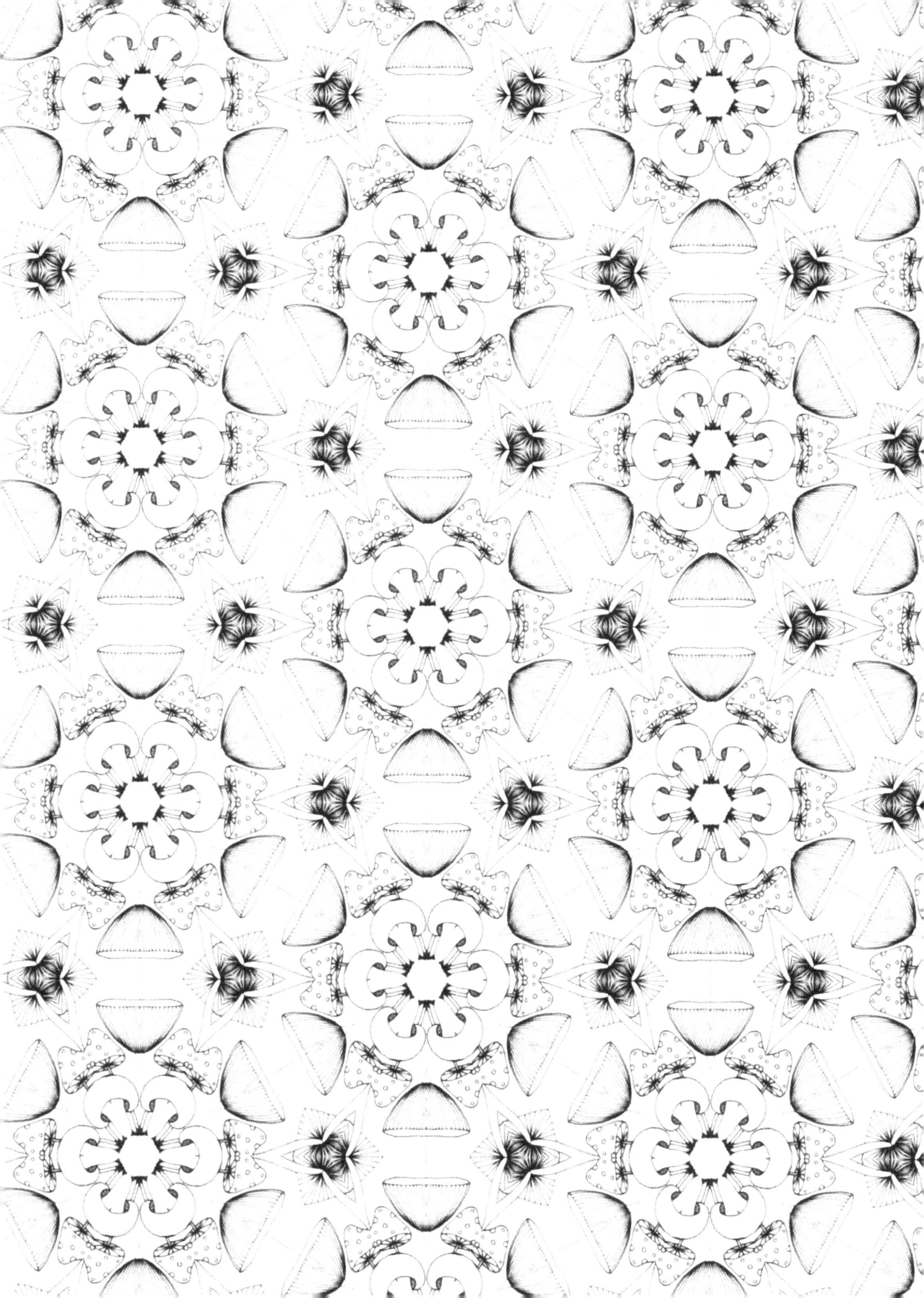

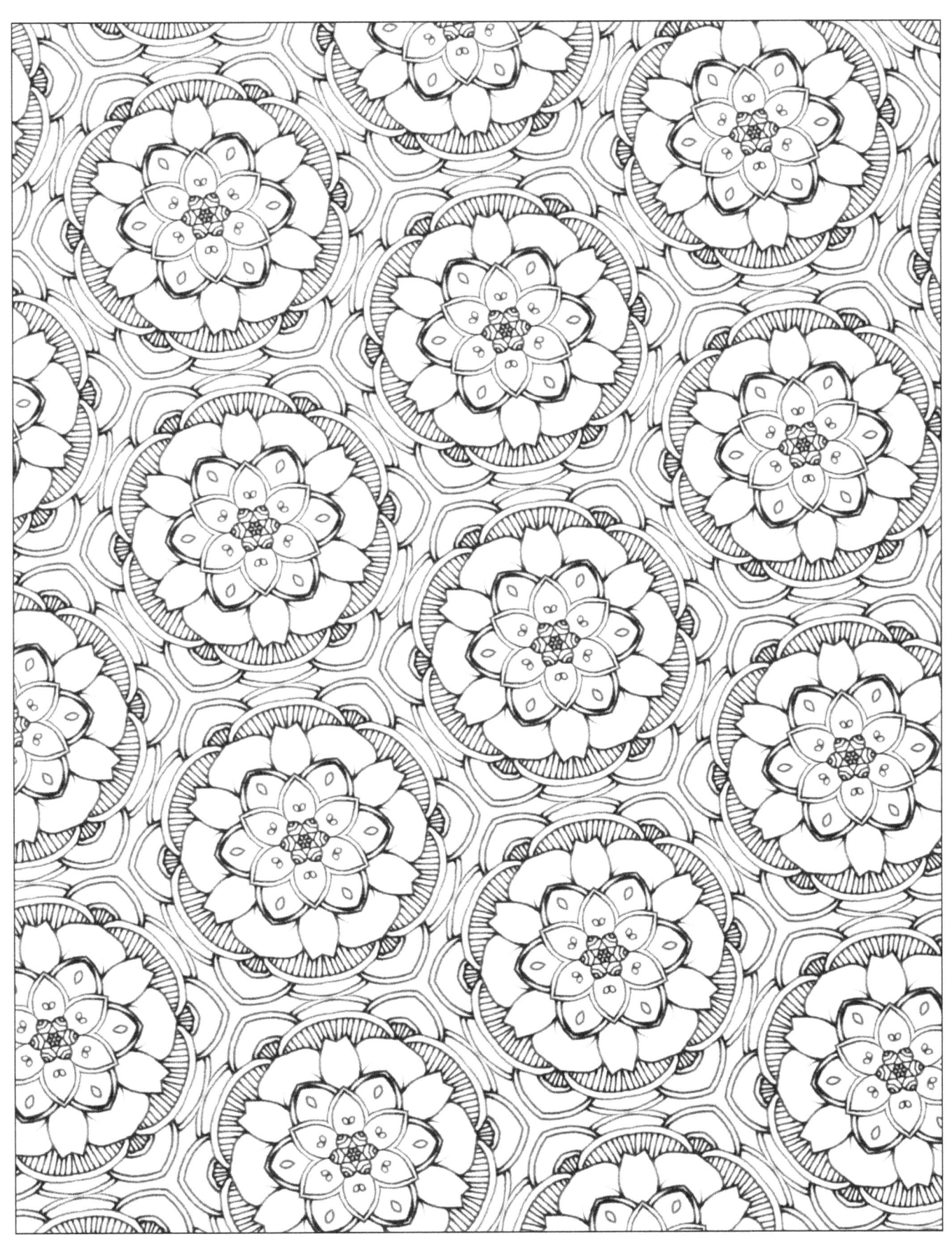

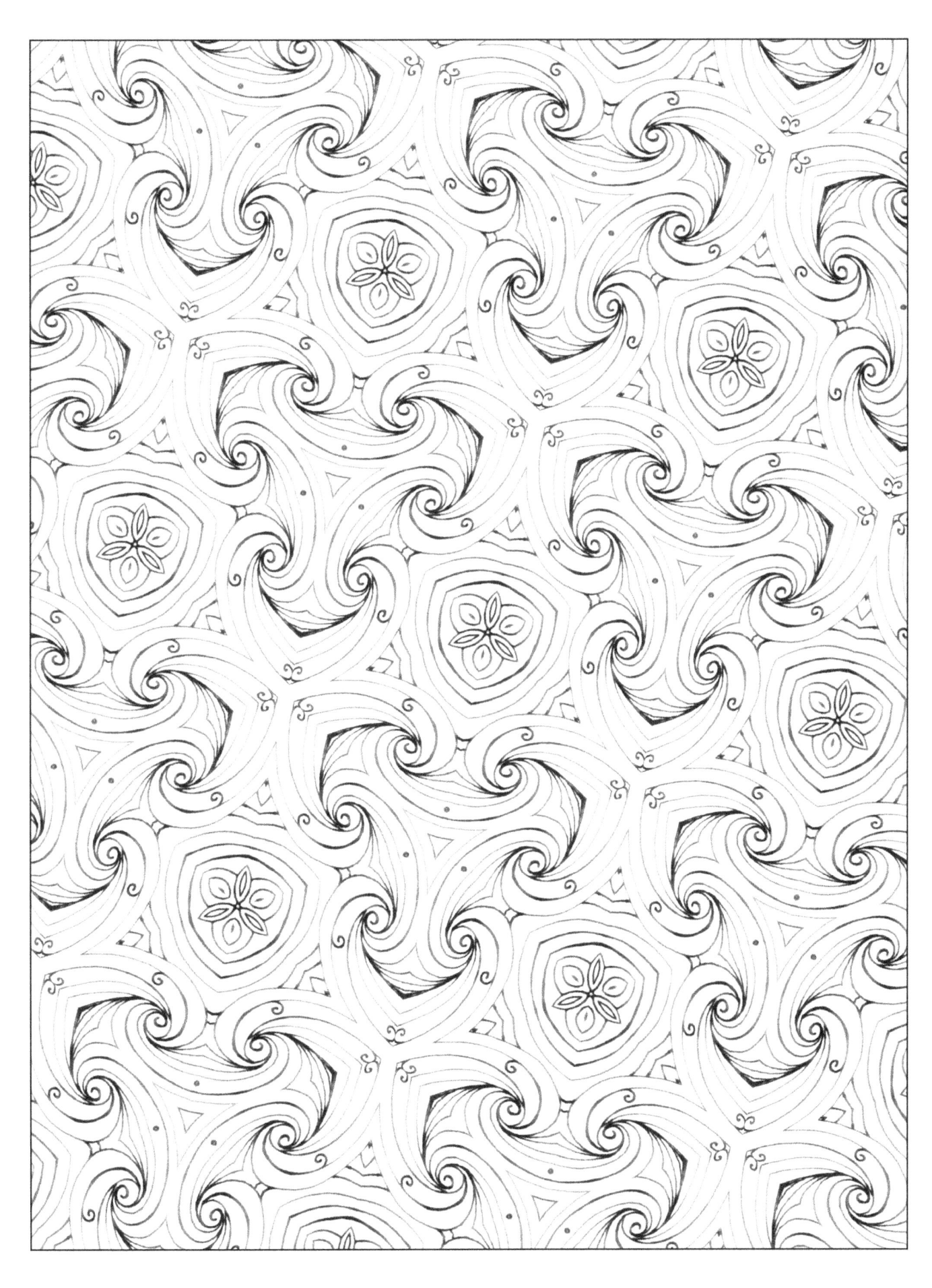

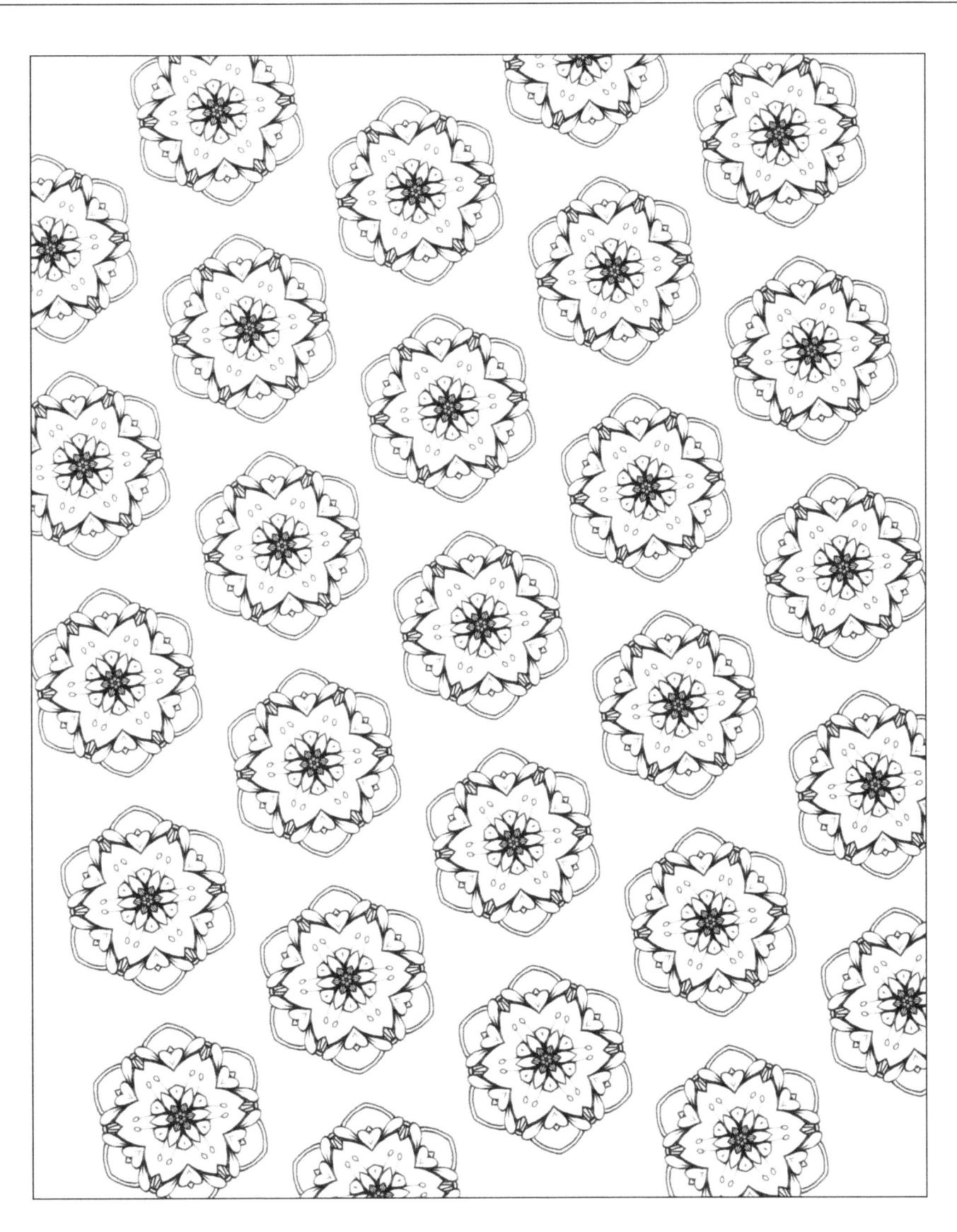

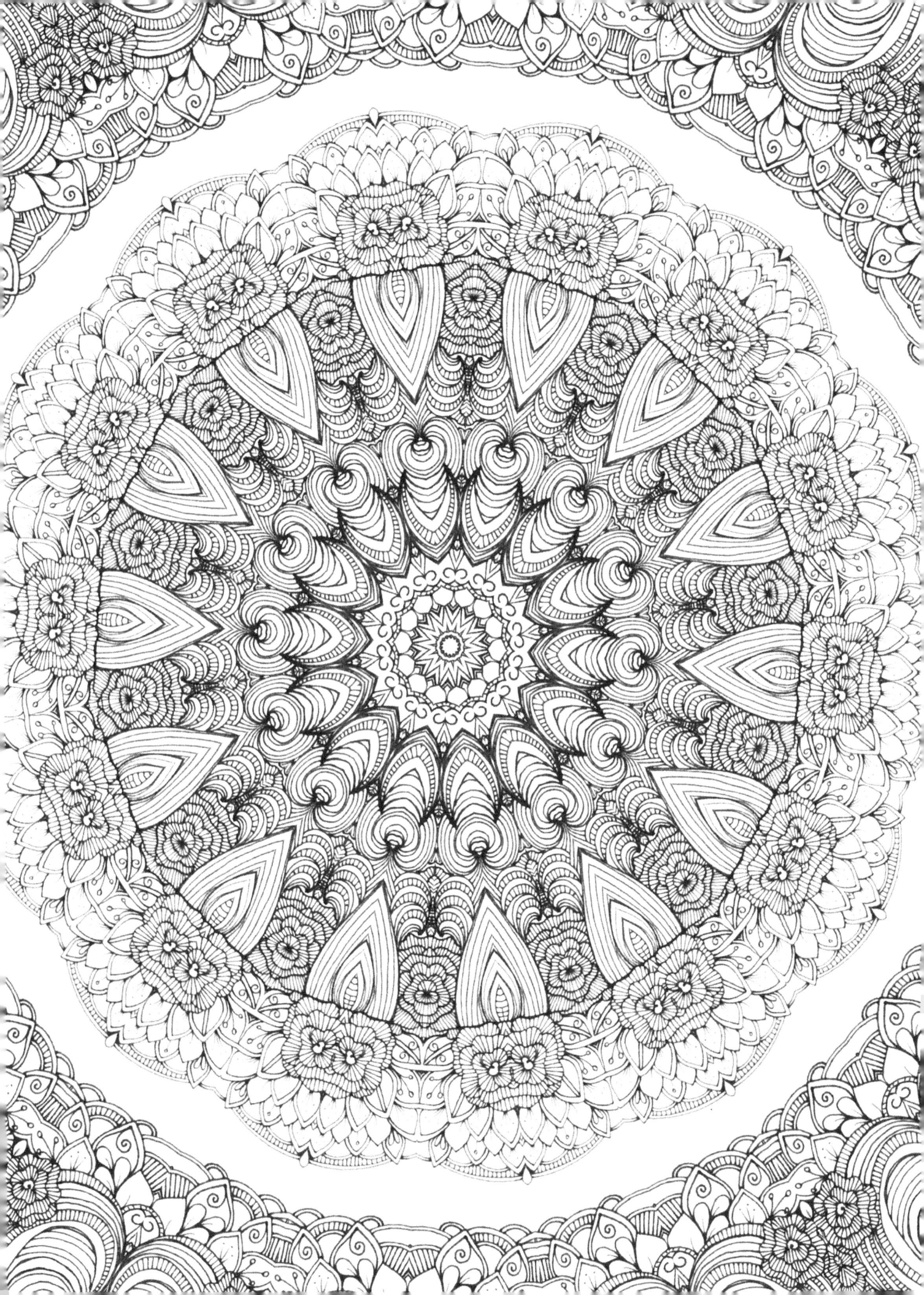

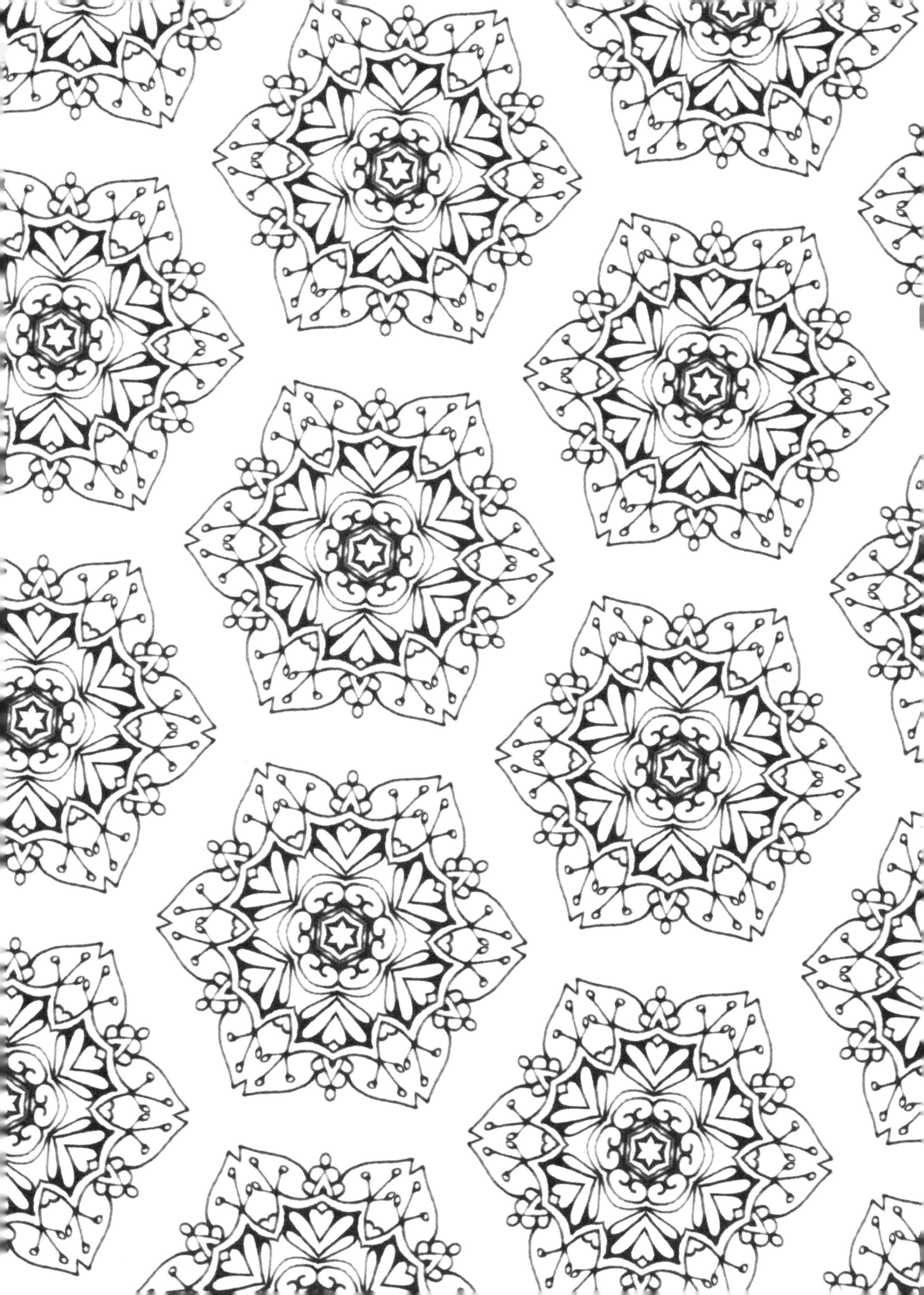

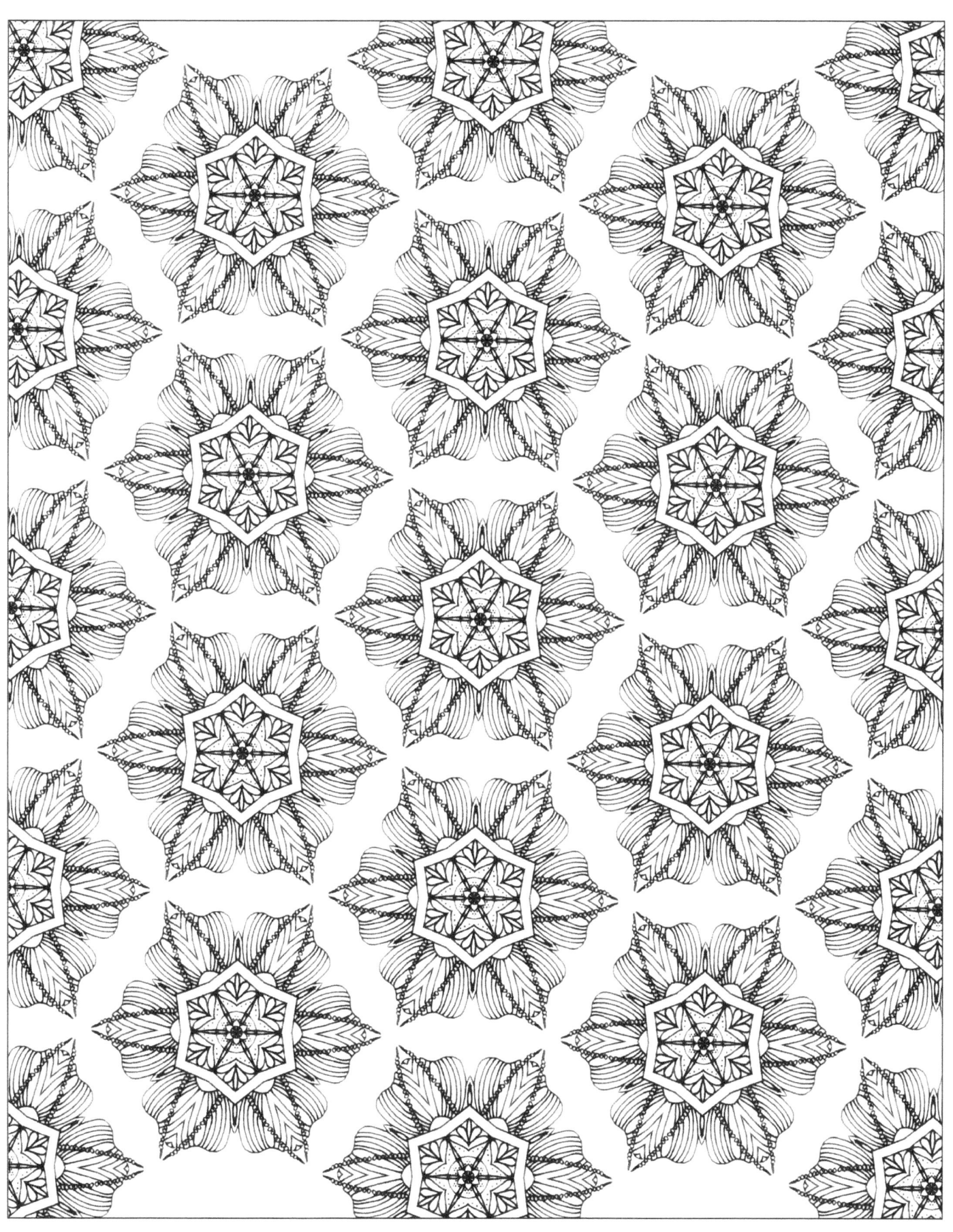

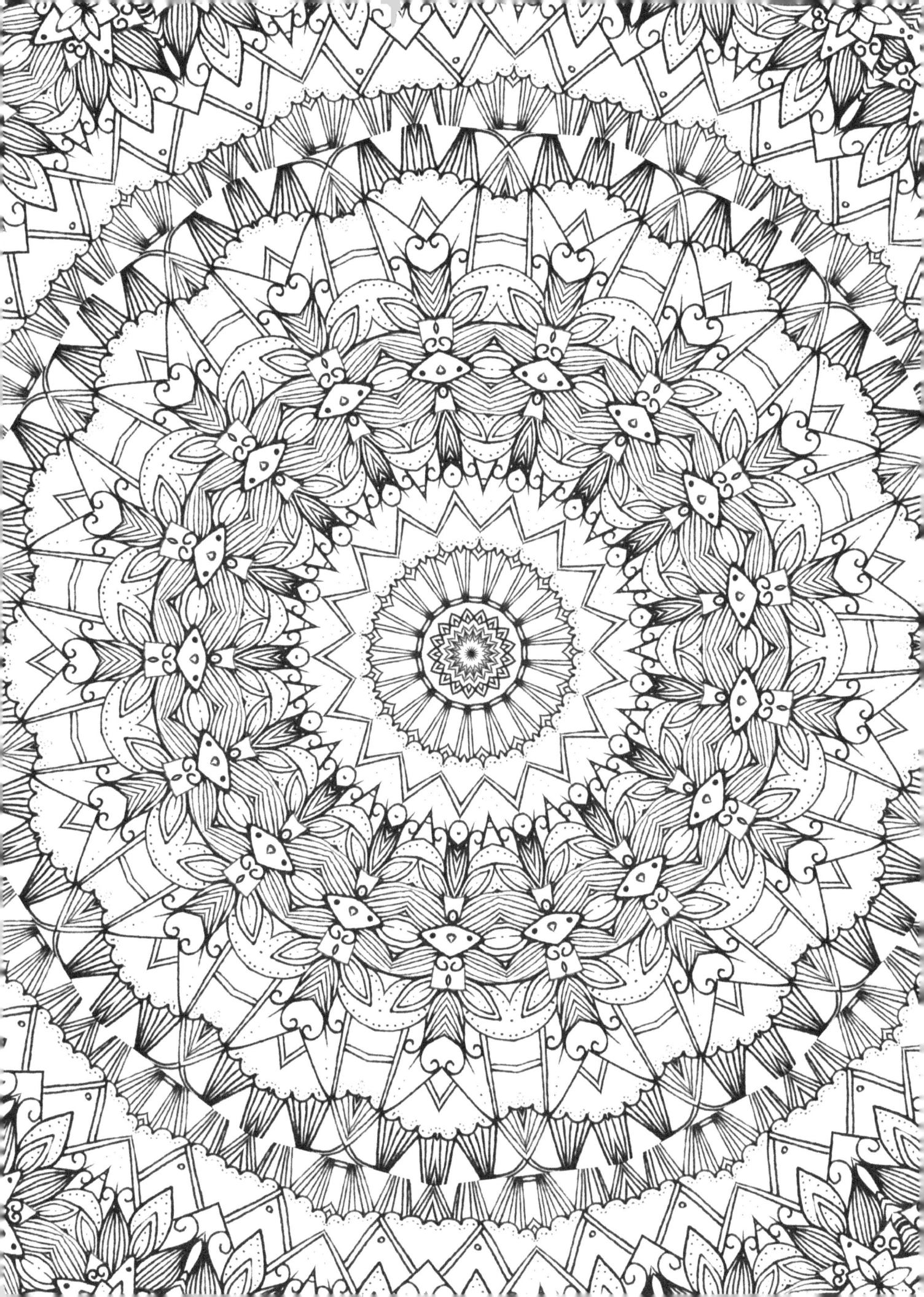

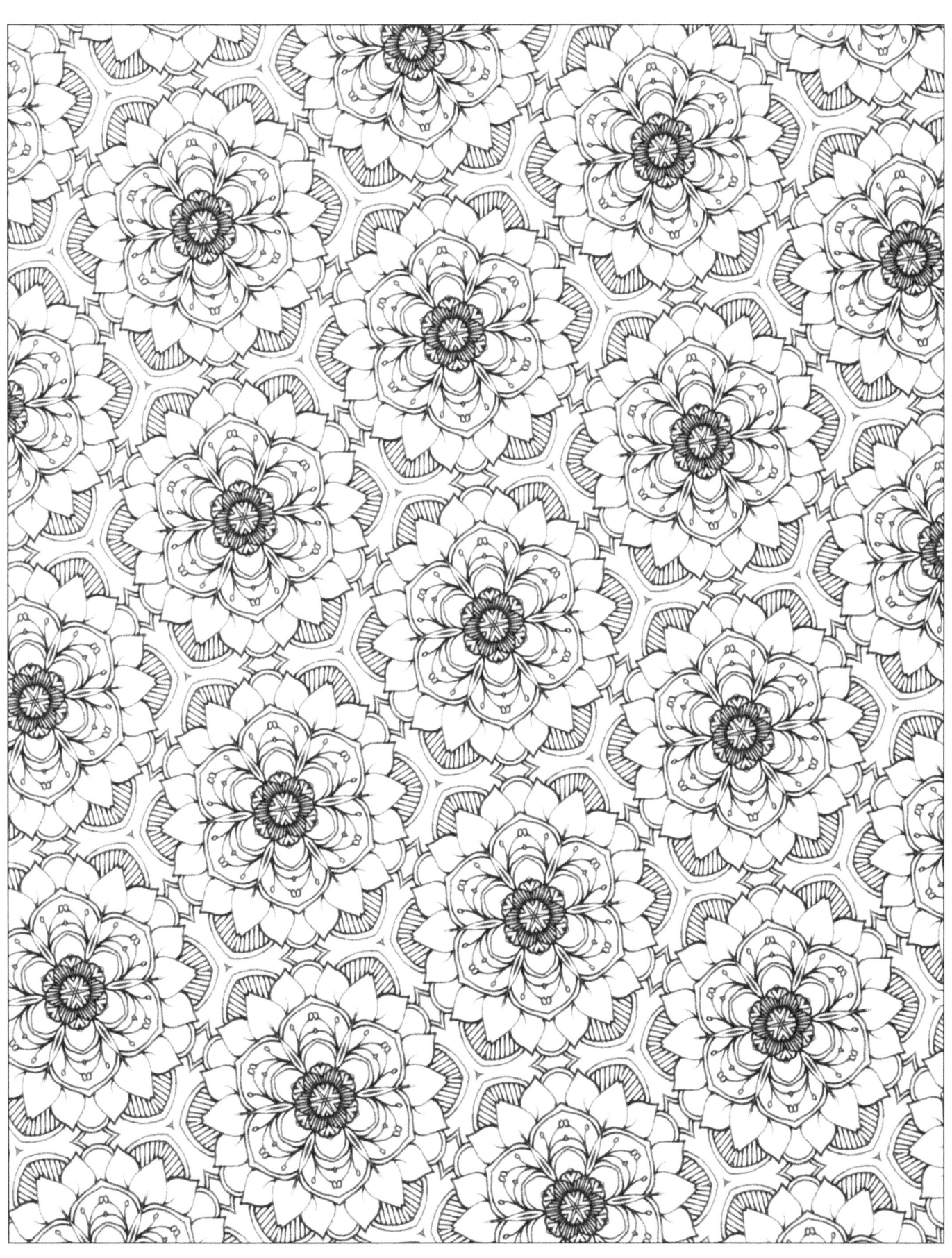

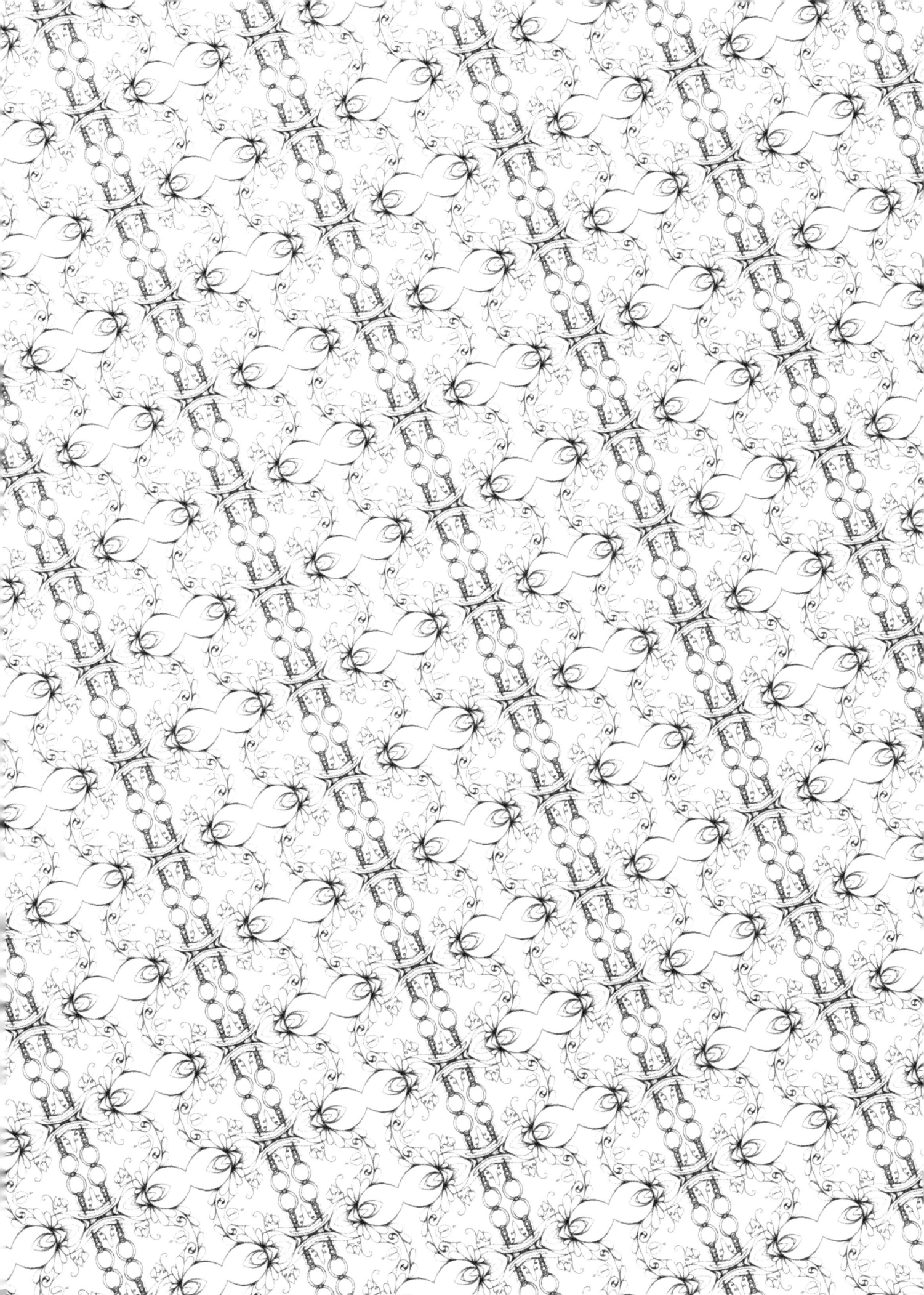

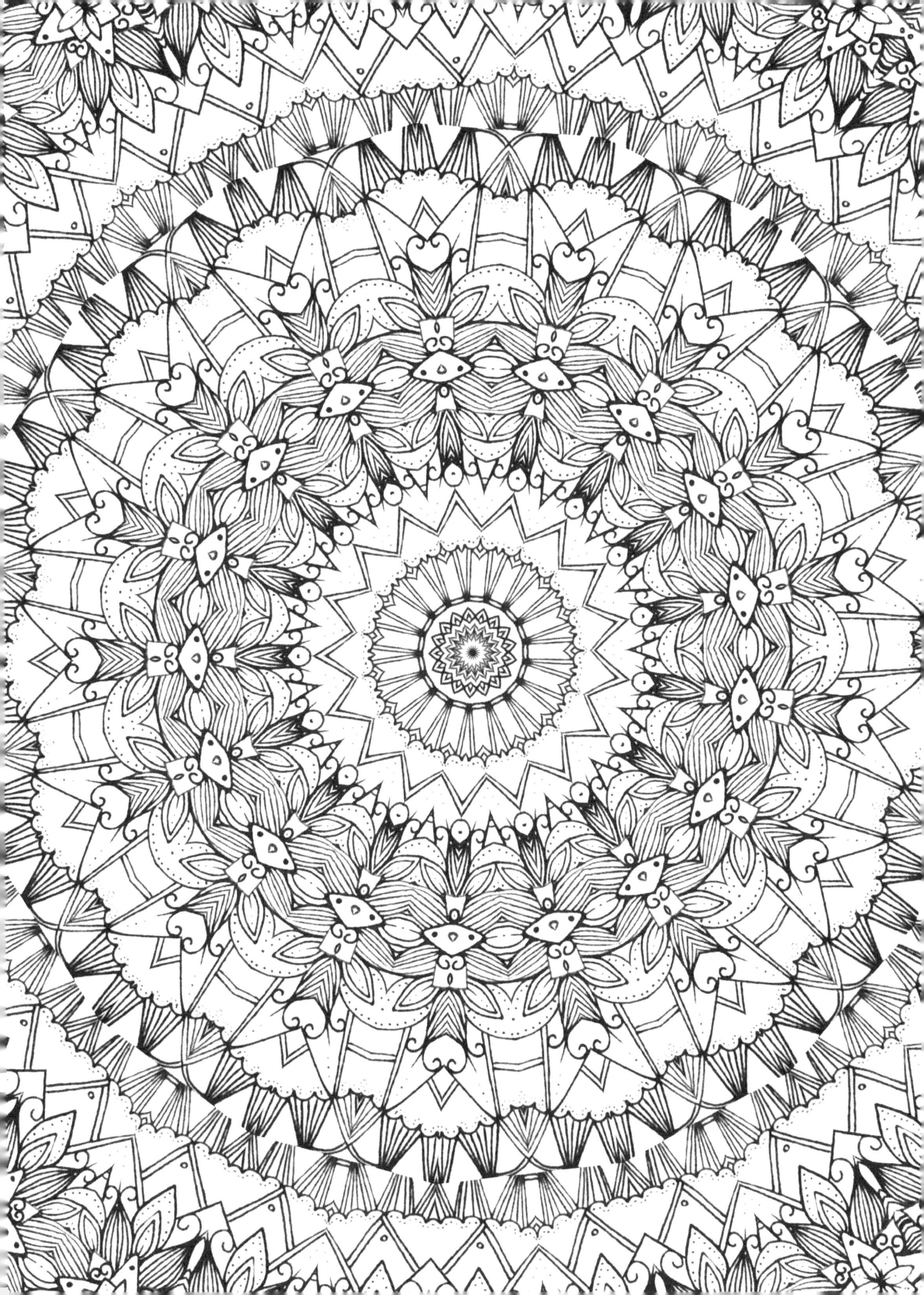

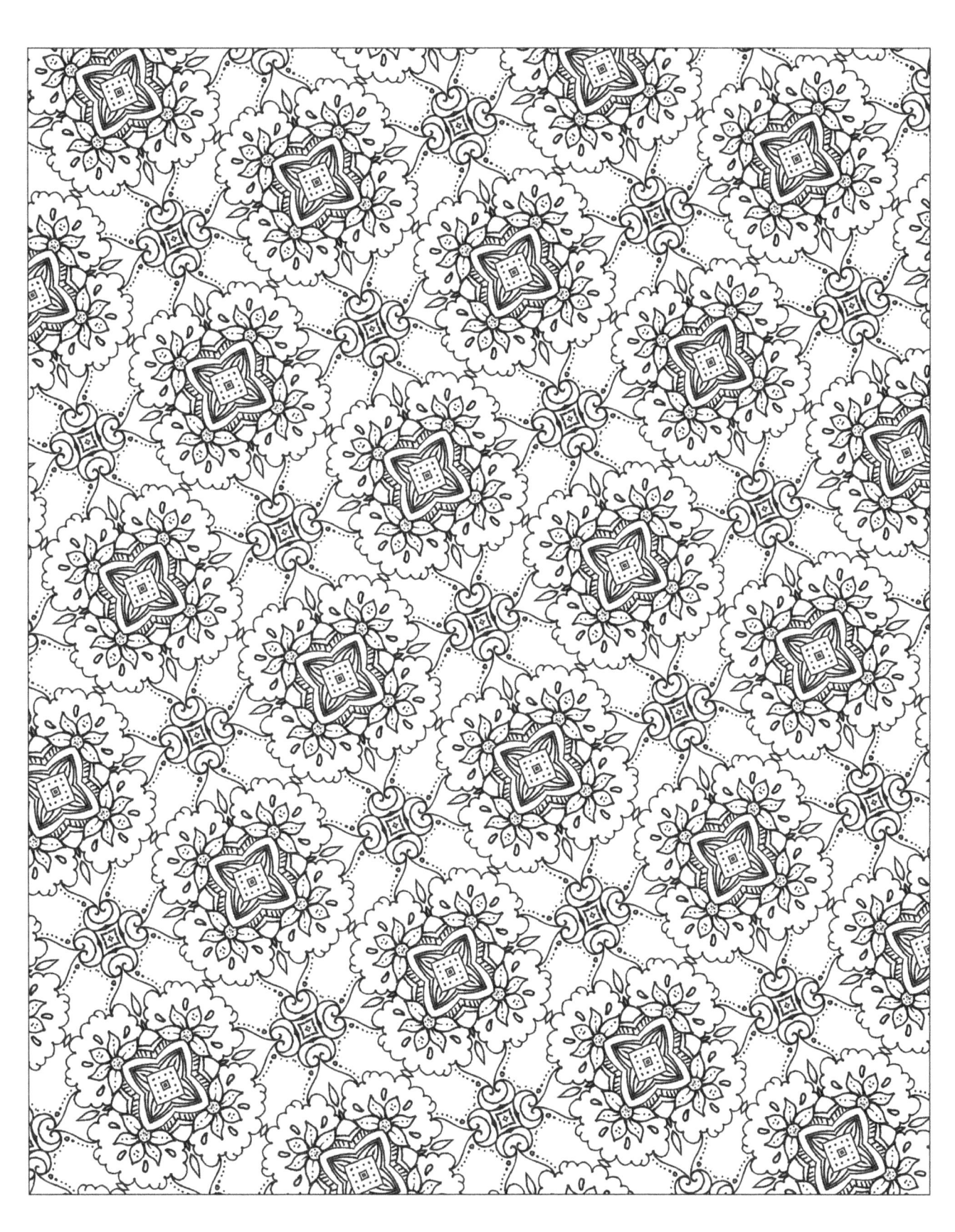

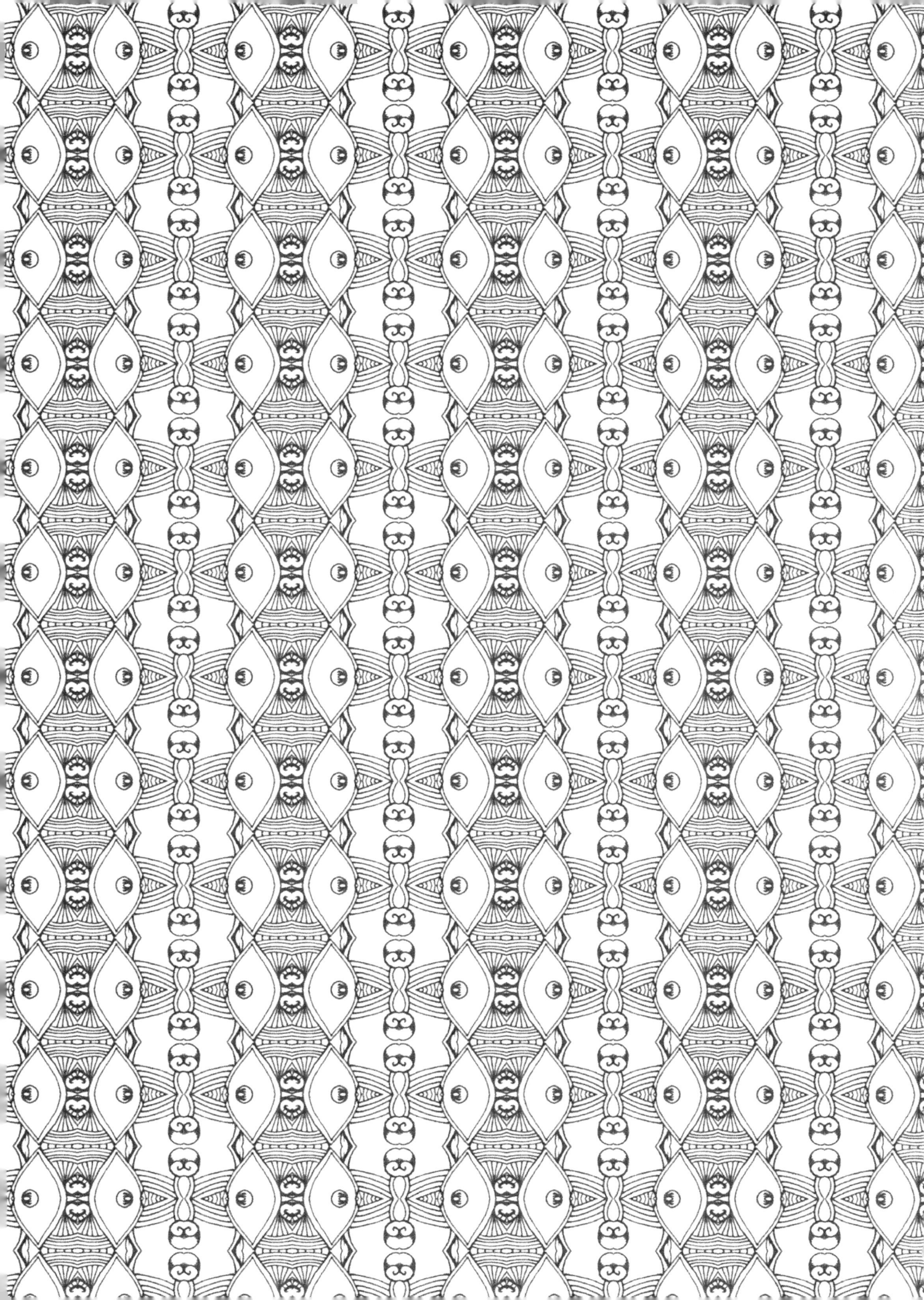

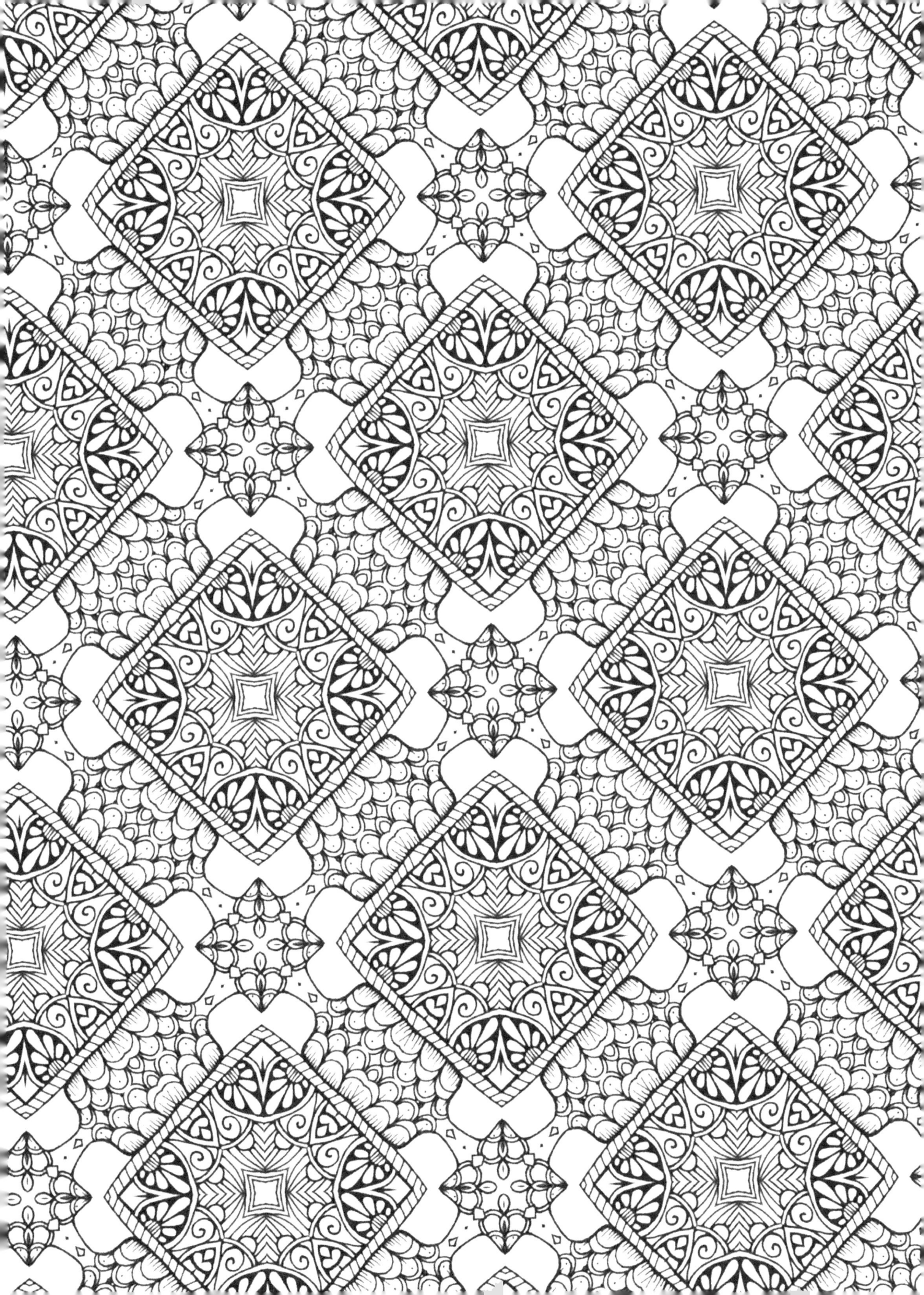

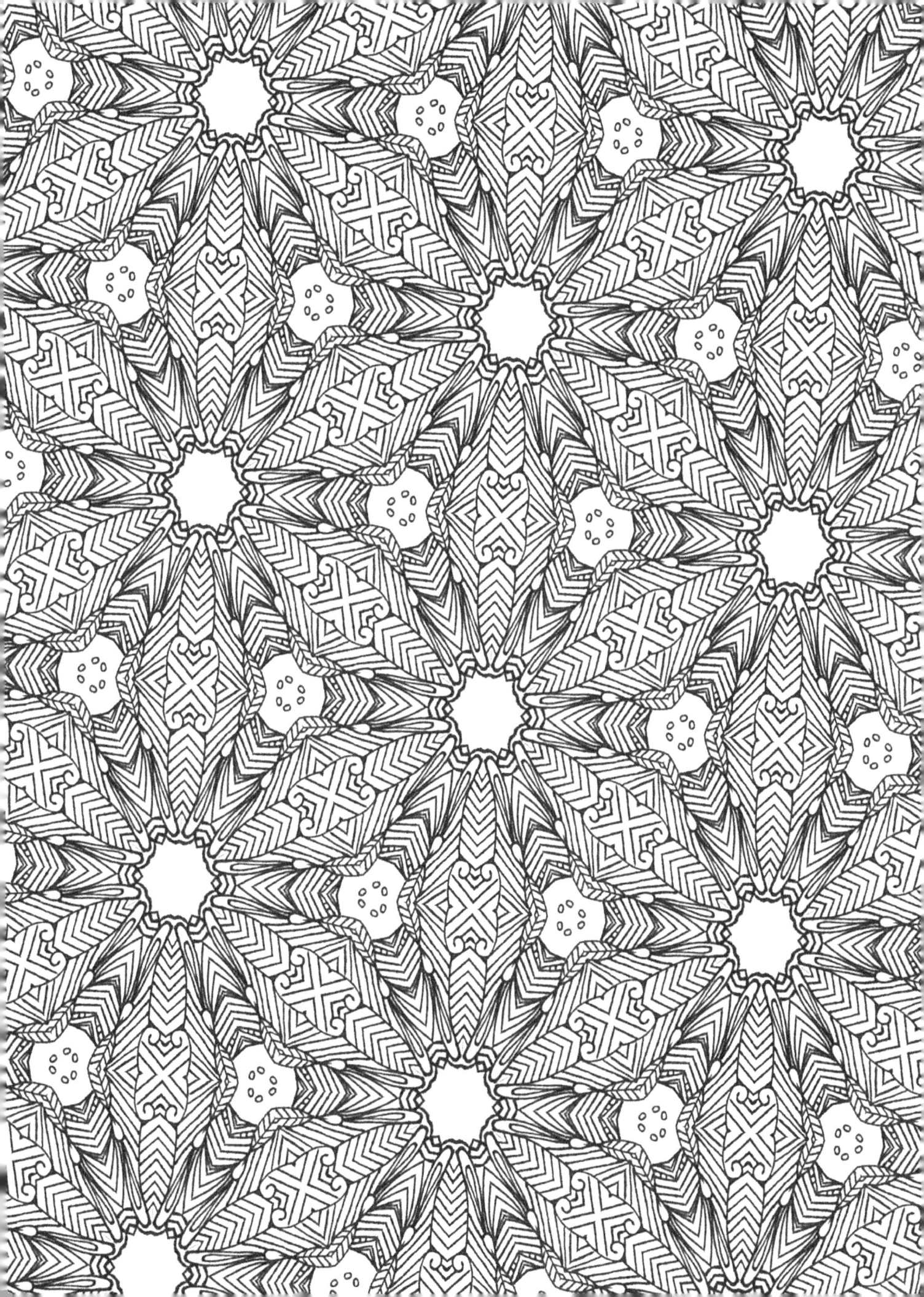

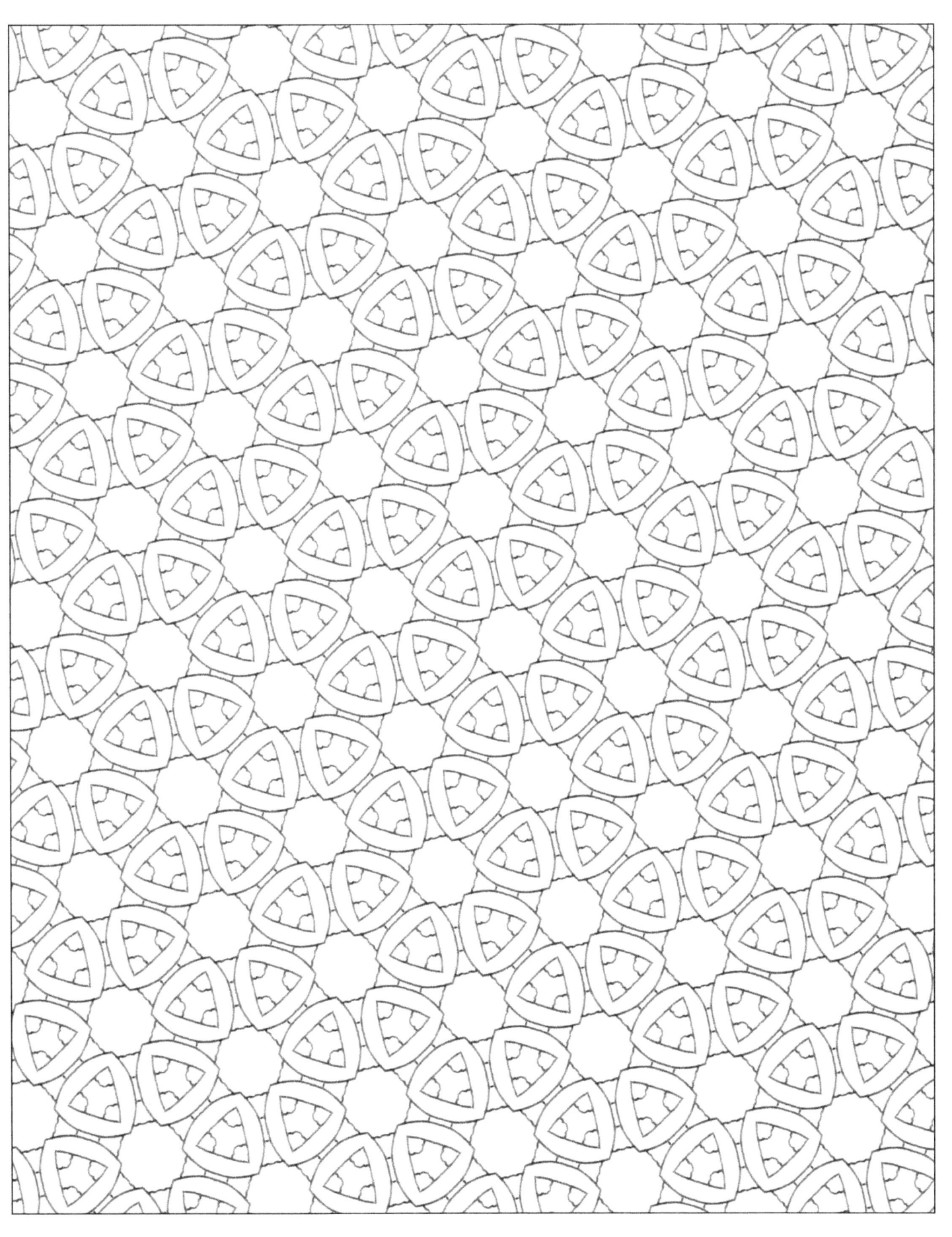

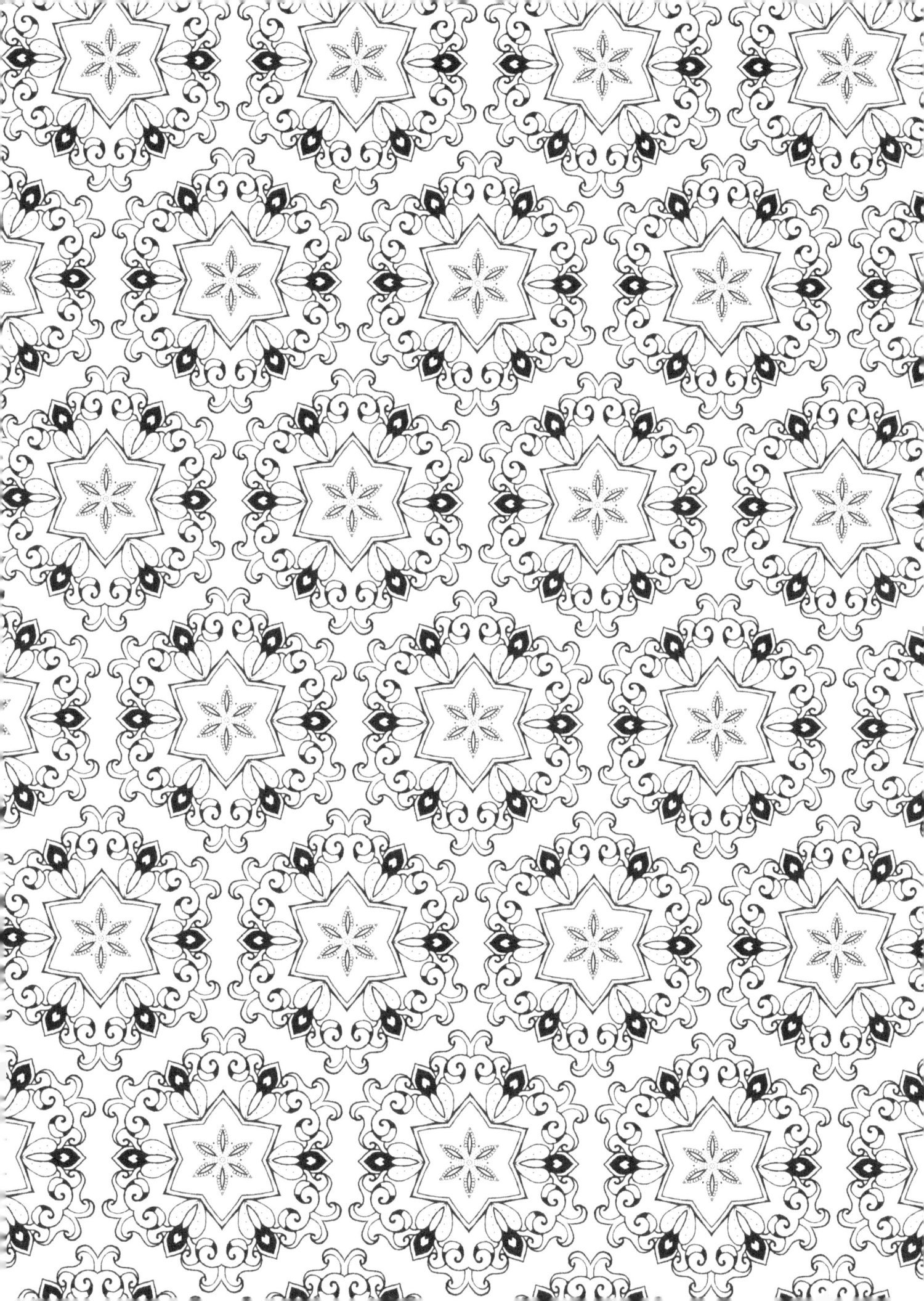

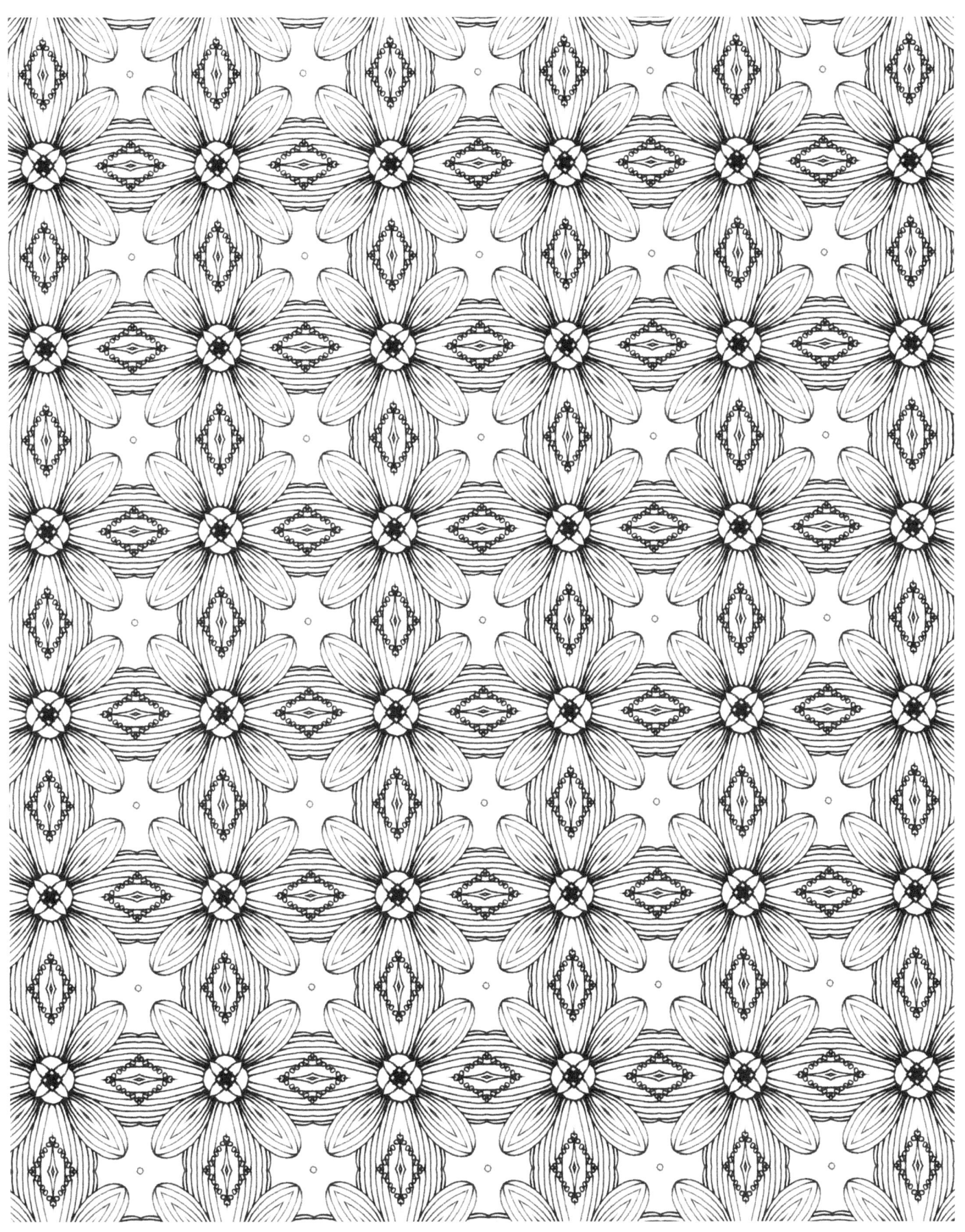

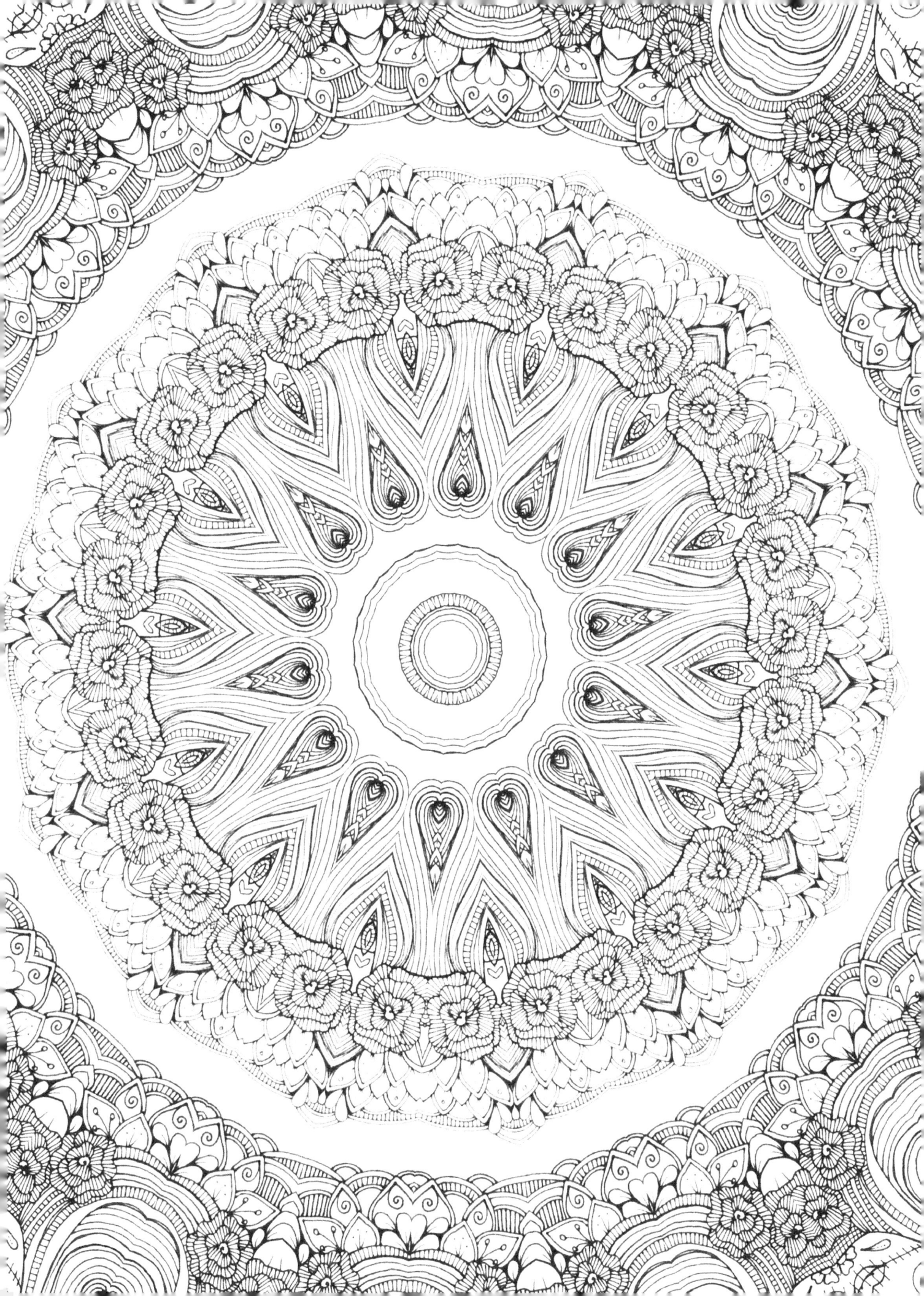

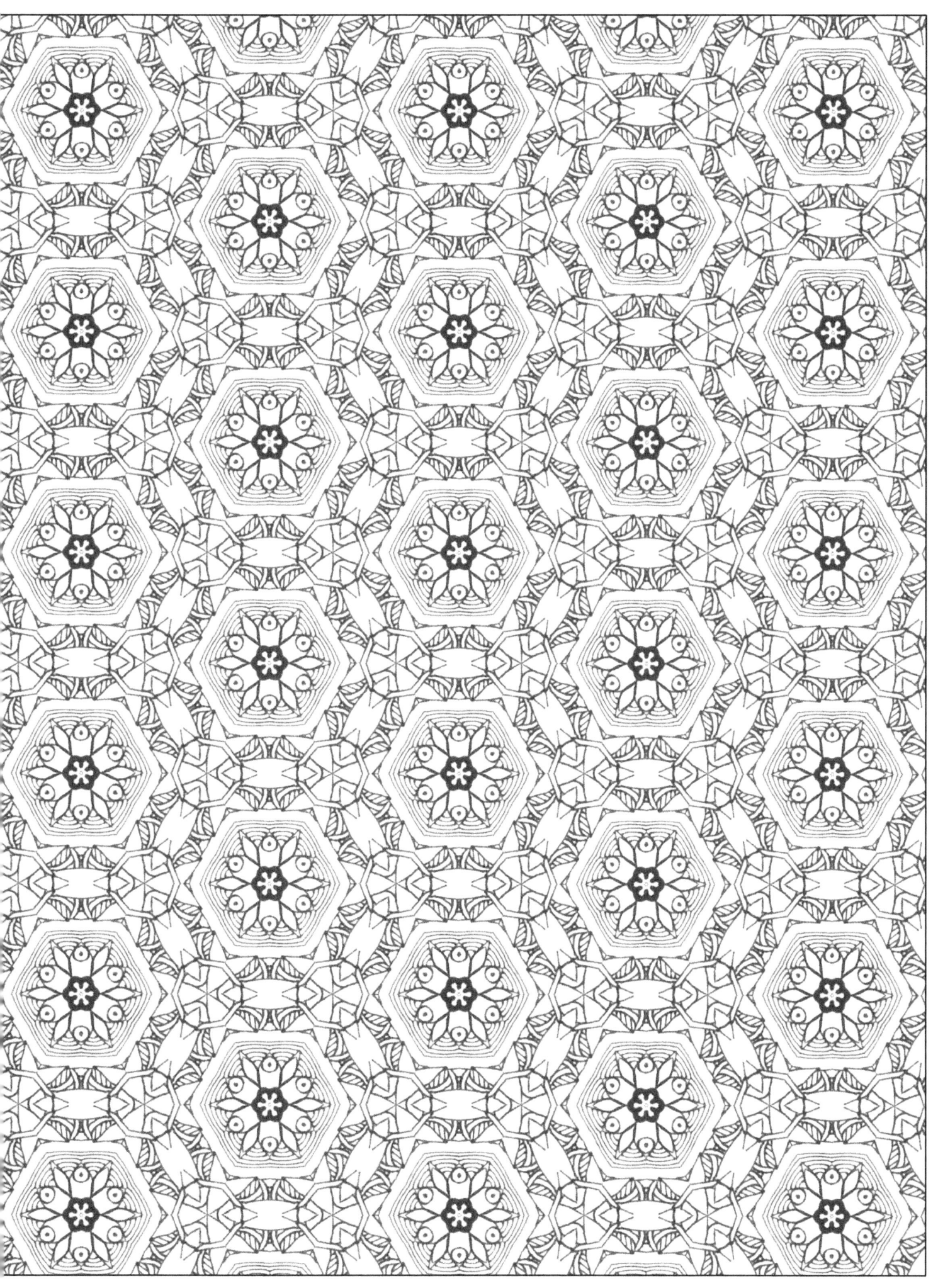

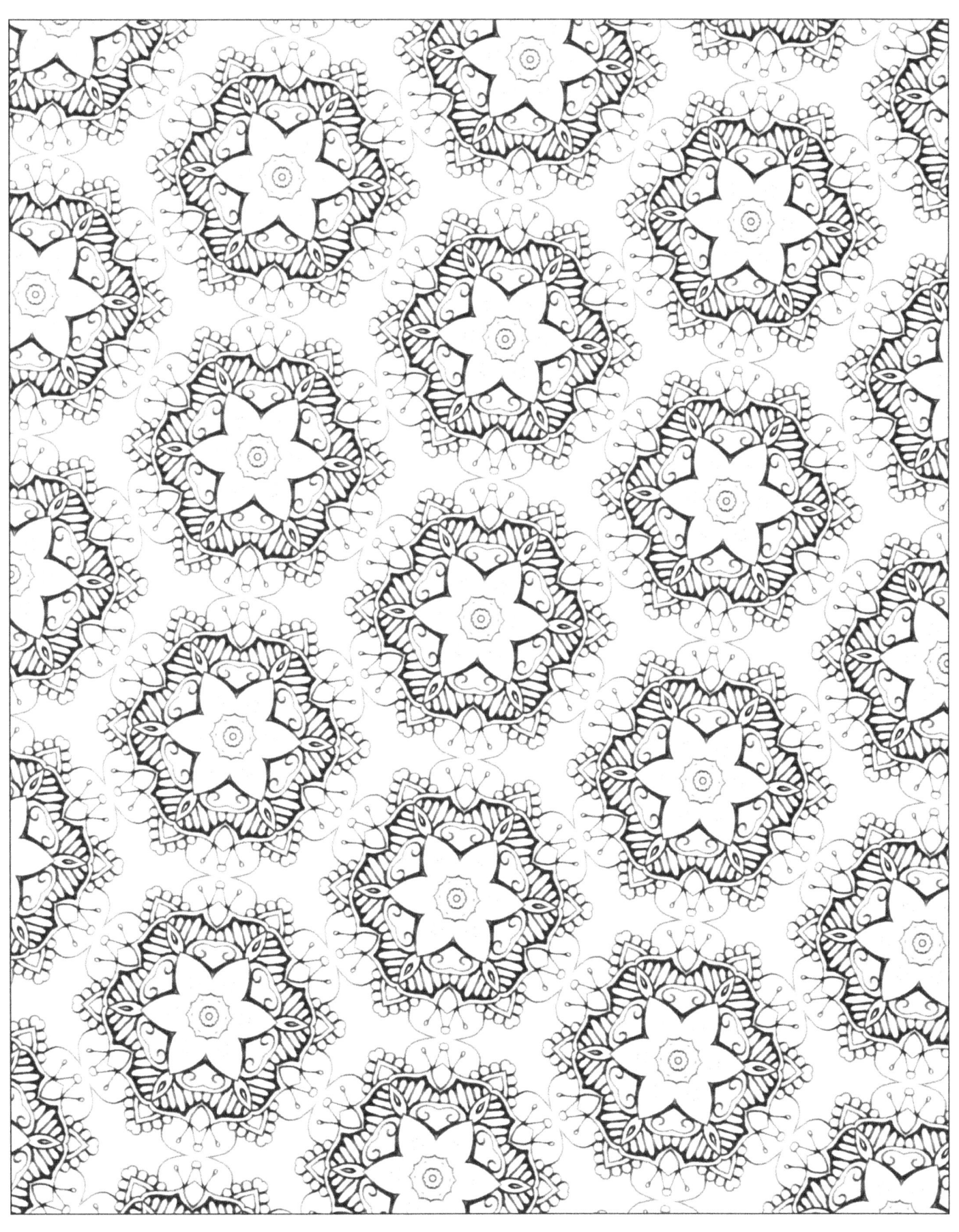

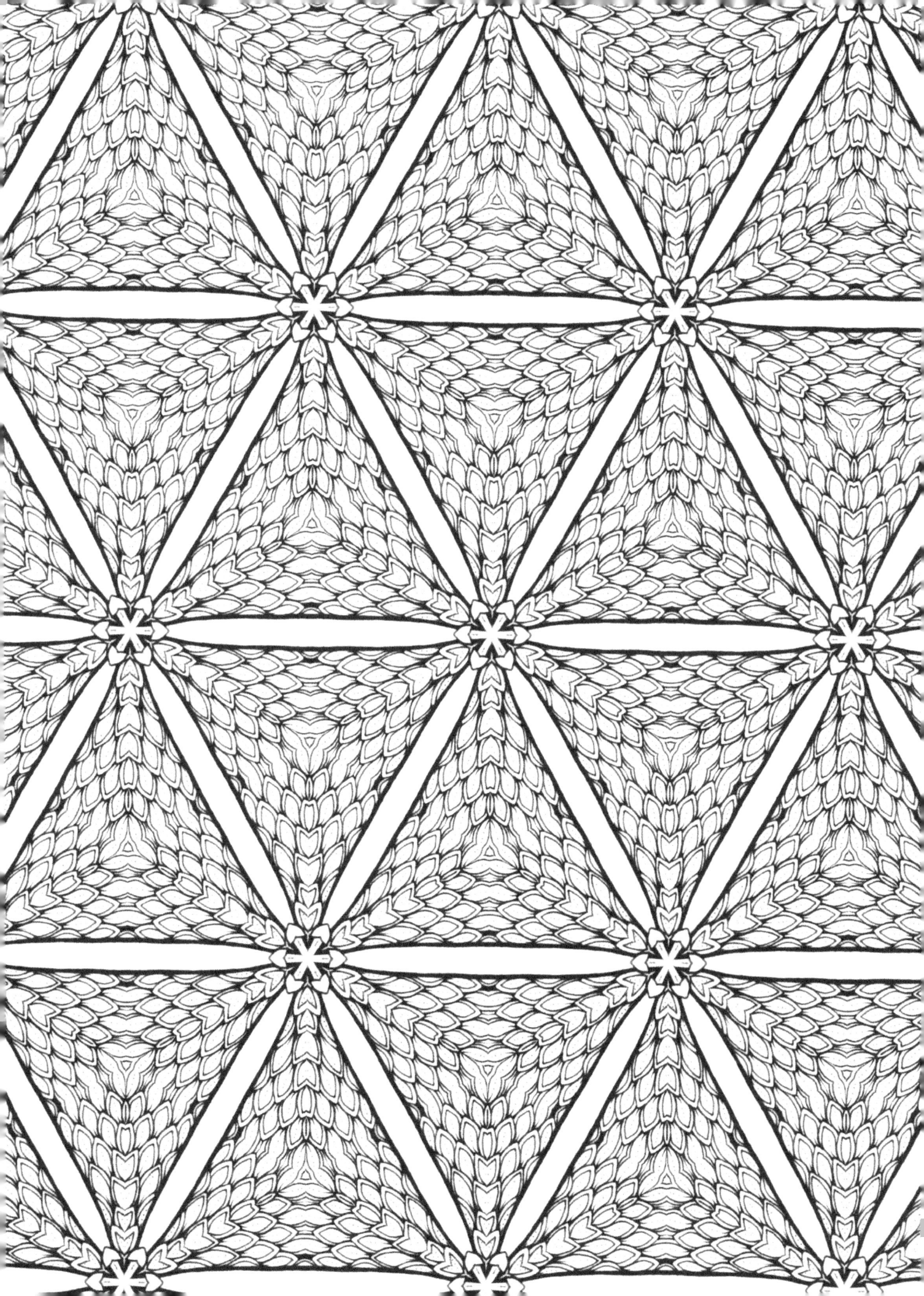

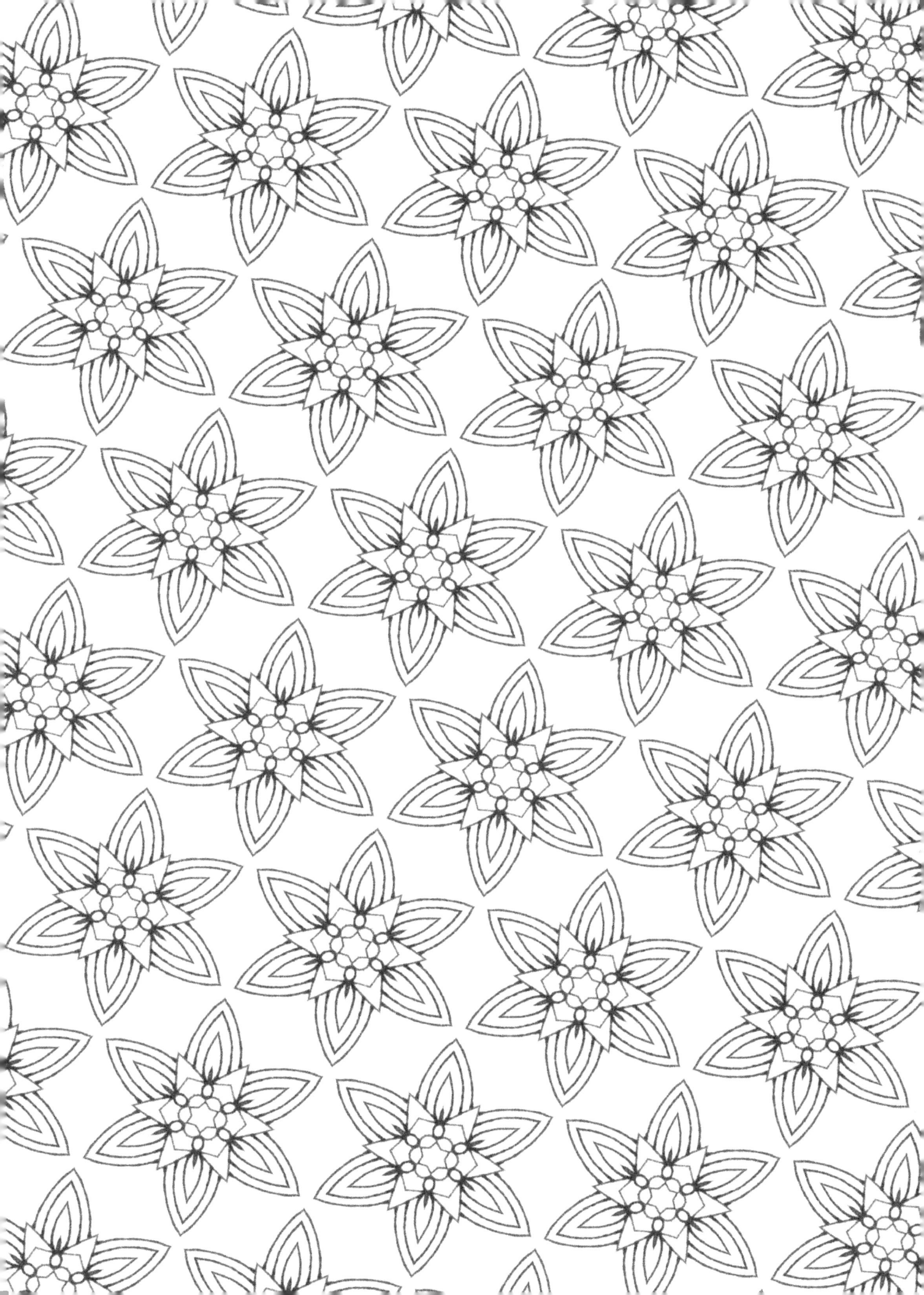

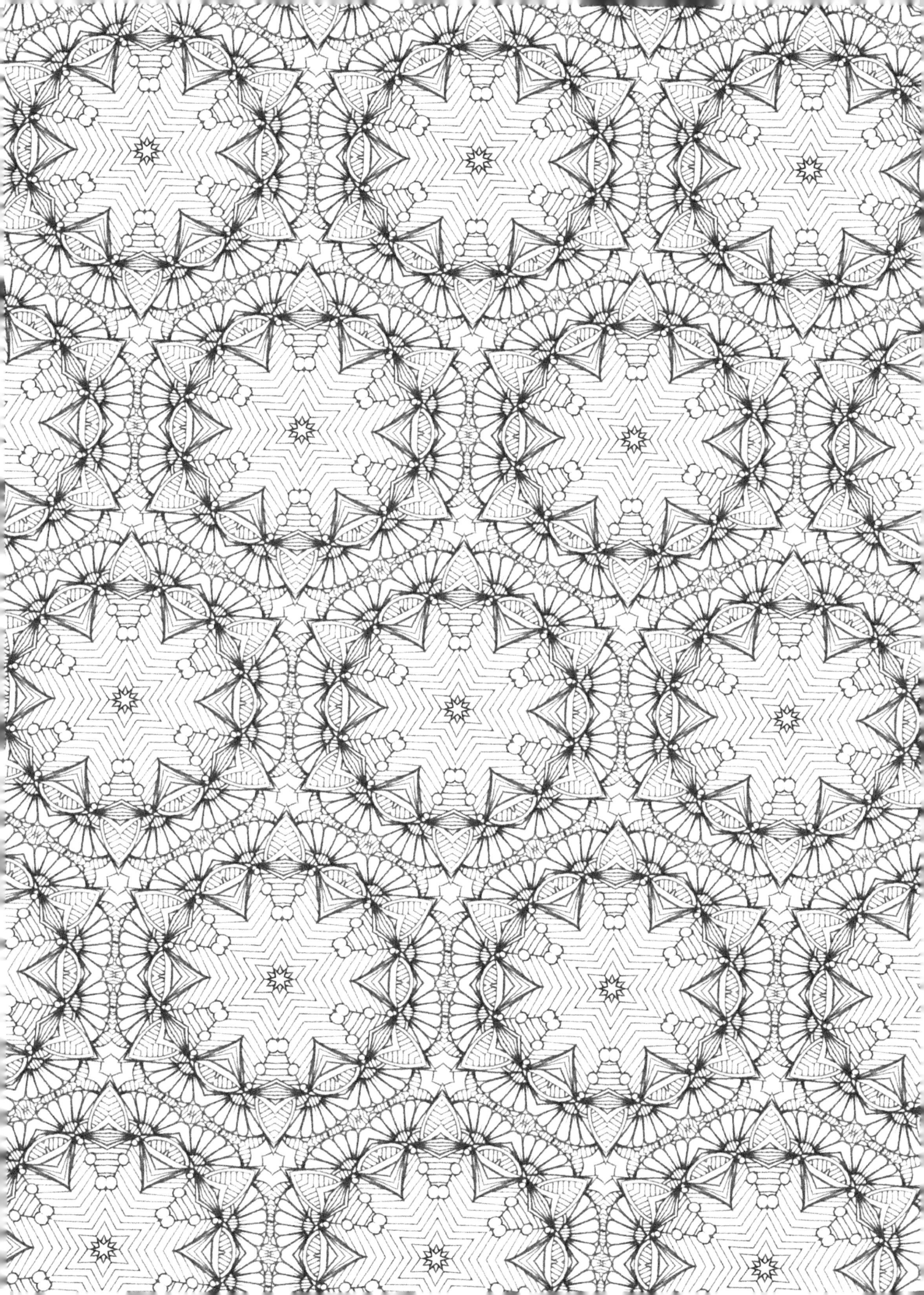